God's Great Trumpet Call

15 Monologues of New Testament People

ROBERT F. SCOTT

CSS Publishing Company, Inc.
Lima, Ohio

GOD'S GREAT TRUMPET CALL

Scripture quotations are from the *New Revised Standard Version of the Bible,*
copyright 1989, by the Division of Christian Education of the National Council of
the Churches of Christ in the USA. Used by permission.

Library of Congress Cataloging-in-Publication Data

Scott, Robert F., 1920-
   God's great trumpet call : 15 monologues of New Testament people / Robert F.
Scott.
      p.   cm.
   ISBN 0-7880-0564-2 (pbk.)
   1. Bible. N.T.—Biography—Sermons. 2. Monologue sermons. 3. Sermons, Ameri-
can. I. Title.
BS2431.S35   1996
225.9'22—dc20   95-39882
                                                           CIP

ISBN: 0-7880-0564-2   PRINTED IN U.S.A.

Blessed be the God and Father
of our Lord Jesus Christ!
By his great mercy he has given us
a new birth into a living hope
through the resurrection of Jesus Christ ...
1 Peter 1:3 (NRSV)

Table Of Contents

Preface

The resurrection of Christ is central in the teaching of the Apostles, and the New Testament gives us sharp vignettes of men and women touched by the risen Christ. Those encounters were tantalizingly brief: they happened to persons whose lives were crowded with thoughts, emotions, families, commitments, friends, community affairs; they were brief events within lifetimes that continued for years afterward.

These 15 monologues explore the possible effect of the Christian faith in the continuing lives of quite diverse individuals, either through their own words or the opinions of persons close to them. I have tried to present them, not as "plaster saints," but as human beings struggling with the reality of Jesus as the divine and living Savior. Obviously, no one can know their exact thoughts, except as their own words are recorded. We can only try to enter into their experiences and empathize with them. Let us therefore speculate, explore, and dream.

A word about inclusive language: our generation has become sensitive to the exclusivism inherent in the constant use of masculine pronouns for God, and I use inclusive language in expressing my own thoughts today. These monologues, however, are an effort to explore the possible thoughts of First Century individuals, to whom inclusive language would have been a totally foreign concept.

My intention is to make the Bible come alive to people, thus stimulating them to further study and deeper faith. There are a few deliberate anachronisms: a television-like switch in a Roman theatre, a new Pontiac in the story about Simon.

7

I have used this device sparingly, but I think that at times it helps to make a bridge to present reality. It is my hope that these studies may stimulate other efforts to bring the people of the Bible to life. I hope, also, that some readers will be inspired to adapt these monologues to dialogues or full-cast dramas.

Some of these character studies were first presented in the Lower Brandywine Presbyterian Church of Wilmington, Delaware, and others were first presented in the Chapel of Ingleside Retirement Apartments, Wilmington, Delaware. I thank both congregations for their encouraging comments. I am indebted to Mr. Thomas W. Lentz and Mrs. Teresa Rhoads of CSS Publishing Company for their editorial advice. I most deeply appreciate the supportive suggestions of my wife Bettie, who has patiently reviewed these studies in various stages of development.

Robert F. Scott

Luke 8:1-3
John 20:1-2, 10-18

Mary Magdalene:
Liberated Woman

Medieval legends confused three women: the sinful "woman of the city" in Luke 7, Mary of Bethany, and Mary Magdalene. In time, "Magdalene" became a synonym for a prostitute. The plain text of the Bible treats each of these three women separately. Mary Magdalene is mentioned by name 12 times in the Gospels, but not once is there a whisper to connect her with the harlot of Luke 7. In recent decades there has been fanciful speculation that Mary was Jesus' wife or mistress. Again, there is not a single word in the whole Bible to support such wild imagination.

After we liberate her from false identification, who was she? What might be her story?

*   *   *

You ask who I am
    and why I constantly speak of Jesus,
        why I call him my savior and my deliverer?

I am Mary from Magdala,
    and I am also a new person,
      liberated and redeemed.
    Jesus the Messiah has given me a new freedom,
    and through him I am alive,
      a child of the living God.

You ask what this means?
I was not always free.
    True, I was nobody's slave,
      I was never in prison,
        the moneylenders had not tangled me
        in their snares.
    My husband loved me,
      provided for me,
        cared for me,
          and trusted me;
      he gave me full liberty
        to come and go as I pleased.
    You see me now, a widow,
      free to go where I wish,
        spend my money as I desire,
          do what I want to do.
Yet once I was not free.
    My bondage was within me,
      a living part of me.
    Forces out of control surged over me,
      as if seven demons lived inside me,
        tearing me to shreds;
    sometimes I thought that I myself was a demon,
      determined to destroy myself
      and everyone I loved.
    One minute I would lash out at my family,
      say words that stung those whom I loved most
      and who loved me;
      the next second I would dissolve into tears,
      hate myself for what I had done.

I was in bondage to my possessions,
  envious of those who had more,
    greedy for things I did not need.
  It's good that my husband was well-to-do;
    my insistent demands
      would have ruined a less prosperous man.
I was ridden by fear,
  fear that people hated me,
    fear my family would scorn me,
      fear of what would become of me.
In time, I feared I was losing my mind,
  and I feared I was so evil
    that God must hate me.
I was torn by hatred,
  nursed thoughts of vengeance
    for every little grievance —
  and — worst of all —
    I knew that was wrong,
      and I hated myself for it.

What transformed me?
The change began when my husband wanted
    to be in Jerusalem for the Feast of Tabernacles.
I went grudgingly,
    complaining of every inconvenience on the way.
At the Temple a crowd was gathered around Jesus.
  We had heard of him as a north-country teacher
    with strange healing powers.
  In curiosity, I listened:
    "If you continue in my word ...
      you will know the truth,
        and the truth will make you free ...
      everyone who commits sin is a slave to sin ...
        if the Son makes you free,
          you will be free indeed."
The words sank in.
  I knew how horrid had been my words,

my thoughts,
     my constant bitterness and complaining.
I knew they were sin,
     and I loathed myself for them.
I knew I was a slave to the feelings I despised,
     and I wanted to be free ... free!
I looked again at Jesus.
     "If the Son makes you free,
     you will be free indeed."
My soul felt a trickle of warmth,
          melting the icy crust of self-centeredness;
     then a stream,
          washing away fear and greed and bitterness;
     then a flood,
          overwhelming the demons
          and sweeping them out in a rushing torrent
               of God's grace.
I listened again to Jesus.
     I felt the love of God,
     and I knew that I was free.

What happened then?
I went home, a new person to my family.
     The rage, the fears,
          the pettiness that had marred our marriage
          were gone.
     I thank God that in those last few months,
          I was able to express my love to my husband;
          at long last I could try to be the wife
          such a good man deserved.

When my husband died,
          what did I have to live for?
     The truth,
          the truth embodied in Jesus,
               had set me free.

I was liberated from the demons of my past;
    surely God had some purpose
        for my new freedom.
In Israel it has long been considered an honor
        to support a Rabbi;
    I had the means to help Jesus and his band.
I could learn from Jesus,
    tell others of Jesus,
        and at times travel with Jesus.

I was not alone, of course.
    There were several of us,
        women of means,
            who owed so much to our teacher.
Joanna was the wife of Herod's steward;
    her husband sent generous gifts
        when she travelled with us.
Susanna brought money of her own.
Usually four or five women
    travelled with Jesus and his twelve;
we bought the food, cooked, washed, learned ...
    and we were able to comfort the women
        of the villages,
    enter their homes
        and tell them the good news of Jesus.

Those months were a time of growth.
    It was hard work but good work,
        walking from town to town,
        rejoicing with new disciples,
        praising God when people were healed,
        always learning when Jesus taught.
Then came that strange foreboding
        on the road from Galilee to Jerusalem,
            when Jesus said those odd words
                we could not understand,
        words about betrayal

and death
and rising again.
All that was forgotten
in the glorious march into Jerusalem,
shouts acclaiming him as Son of David,
Messiah.

We were crushed and broken on that terrible day
when he was arrested,
condemned,
crucified.
Even then we could not leave him,
As his body hung on the cross,
we huddled together:
his mother,
Salome,
Mary the mother of James,
and I.
We heard his last words;
we wept when he died.
How we longed to take him down,
at least to give him a decent burial;
the soldiers barred the way;
we did not dare touch him.

We watched at a distance as two strangers
and their servants carried him away.
Who were those men,
so richly dressed and with such authority?
We did not yet know that
Joseph of Arimathea and Nicodemus
were secret believers;
we did not know the roles they would take
in the church
and the prices they would pay.
We kept our distance,
followed them secretly,
saw where they placed him in a tomb.

There had been no time to anoint Jesus' body
        in the proper way.
    After the Sabbath,
        as soon as the shops were open,
        we bought spices.
    Early in the morning we went to the tomb,
        brokenhearted.
    Then the sunlight of God flooded our souls,
        and life changed forever.
    The tomb was open,
        empty,
        and an angel said Jesus had risen!
    We ran to the disciples.
    Then I returned.
        I was standing in the garden,
                near the tomb,
            when Jesus came to me
                and called me by name.
    It was he!
    He had risen, as he said!
    He was alive!

Why should I be the one to see him first?
    Why not his mother, or John, or Peter,
        or all of the twelve?
    Was it pure chance,
        or was it a special honor
        that I should be the first to shout with joy?
    For I did shout!
        "I have seen the Lord!"
    I shouted it to the disciples.
    I shouted it to his mother.
    I shouted it to all the believers.
    I shouted it from the housetops,
        and I shout it to this day.

That was my second liberation.
    When I first met Jesus,

15

he rescued me from the demonic forces
that nearly destroyed me.
When the risen Jesus appeared,
he freed us all from the despair
that had overwhelmed us at the cross.
Now I am living my third liberation, for day by day
Jesus the Christ increases my freedom:
freedom to believe, to hope, to trust;
freedom to rejoice in God;
freedom to praise God for salvation;
freedom to live, to live again and really live!

He is liberating me from all the old barriers
between people.
It began with his little band in Galilee:
Jesus himself, a carpenter's son,
Joanna from the royal court,
fishermen,
a former tax collector.
Jesus set me free to welcome people
for their own inner worth.
He opened me to welcome rich and poor,
slave and free,
men and women,
all equally set free to praise our Savior.
Gentile and Jew now share the bread
of the Lord's supper,
old hatreds set aside by our one salvation.

I am free,
and each new day Jesus sets me free again,
I and everyone else who believes in Jesus:
released from old burdens,
delivered from old cares,
liberated into the joyous service
of Jesus our Lord,
sent out into the world to live our liberation.

Acts 1:15-17, 21-26

The Lot Fell
On Matthias

In the film, The Silence, *a young Mennonite farmer is chosen by lot to be the minister in his congregation, but later he is silenced by his bishop. Ministers are still picked that way among the Amish and some of the old order Mennonites. When it happens to a man, it changes his life drastically. Those ministers do not say, "I was chosen by lot." The usual expressions are "I was hit by the lot" or "The lot fell on me."*

* * *

Why me?
  Out of 120 believers,
      why have they chosen me, Matthias?
  Joseph Barsabbas is a good disciple,
      as good as me and better.

How can I be part of this ministry:
    stand next to Peter and James and John
        and the others who were so close to Jesus?

Oh, I know they did not pick me carelessly.
They prayed for wisdom,
and they looked at us all —
we who had followed Jesus these three years:
not followed on every trip,
like that inner circle of twelve,
but we followed,
listened,
tried to obey.
And we saw him
after he had risen from the dead.
We are witnesses of his life
and his death
and his resurrection.

They chose Joseph and me.
Then they prayed —
asked God to make the final choice —
and they cast lots.
They wrote our names on stones
and put them in a jar.
When they shook the jar,
my stone fell out:
no accident,
for they had prayed for God to rule,
and they depended on God
to show them his choice.

They depended.
Dependence.
That's what it takes to be an apostle.
When Jesus took the twelve and sent them out,
they went without food, money, protection —
depending on God to supply their needs.
Dependence on God became their whole way of life.
They left everything and followed the Master.

Some of us still had our farms
    or some had boats.
We followed him, off and on,
    listening to him,
    telling others of him,
        between farming or fishing.
Now I must leave the farm
    and depend on him alone.

I have a new calling: apostle —
    a witness to the resurrection.
Christ has risen. We have seen him alive.
That is the great, crowning proof.
He is the Messiah!
He is the King!
He is the Lord!
I can feel his power, his energy.
    I feel it in the others.
    I felt it when the lot fell on me!
I must fully depend on him,
    for by the life of the living Christ,
        I am a witness to the resurrection.

So I am taking Judas' place.
I admired Judas,
        one of the chosen twelve.
    He seemed so strong, so sure.
Now he has fallen,
    and I am in his place.
Am I going to fall —
    or stand?
And if I fall,
    will I bring others down?
No!
God forbid!
An apostle must strengthen the believers,
    care for them,
        hold them up.

19

I must depend on Jesus —
on the living, risen Jesus.
I can stand only by his strength,
by his nearness,
by his grace.

This is what it means to live as a disciple.
We have seen him, felt him;
now we must trust him.
He has given us orders to wait —
wait until he gives us his spirit with power,
then obey him in that power.
He has his plan for this world,
and we have his promise
that he will come again in clouds of glory.
Look for that day;
and until that day, encourage each other
with the sure and certain hope of his coming.

What can I do to be a witness to the resurrection?
After Jesus gave us that commission,
he disappeared.
He made it plain we would not see him again
until he comes in glory.
He leaves it to us to show he is alive.
When I stand as a witness,
it must be by my own experience,
my own assurance he is here.
When a witness is in court,
the judge will not accept a secondhand story,
that I have heard about Jesus
or know about Jesus.
It must be my own report,
that I know him,
that I know he is alive,
that he lives in me.

I must have more than words.
My whole life must witness
that I have met the risen Lord.

Jesus said we would be his witnesses in Jerusalem,
in Judea,
in Samaria,
and in all the world.
It's a long way home to Galilee —
and he said Samaria —
those aliens, cultists, heretics —
then the world.
Can he really mean people of other nations?
Other races?

It's no use thinking of the world
unless I start where I am —
Jesus with me here:
Jesus with me in the house where I am lodging,
Jesus with me when I walk on the street,
Jesus with me whenever I meet people today.

I must start with myself:
with my own love for God,
my love for people,
my honesty.
What if Jesus makes no difference in my morality:
if I lie and cheat, steal, lust,
fail to cry out when I see a wrong?
Who then will believe me when I tell of Christ?
Zacchaeus stopped stealing and gave back the money:
my honesty must show that Jesus lives in me.
Let no one point to me and ask
what I would do differently if Jesus were here.
He is here.
I pray the power of his spirit
will let me show he is here.

How shall I witness to the resurrection in my family?
  Yesterday I criticized my wife;
    last night I scolded my daughter.
  My brother will not speak to me:
      he says I've made a fool of myself
      by following Jesus.
  Yet Jesus taught us to love.
  He forgave.
      How humbly I must ask forgiveness —
      from him,
      from my family!
  He has made us to love each other,
    yet husband and wife love and fight,
    are proud of each other
      and disappoint each other —
    and need to forgive in order to heal.
  How we all need the risen Christ with us
    in order to forgive and to heal!

How do I bring the resurrection to the poor?
  Jesus cared for the poor,
    and the early prophets of God
      called out for justice to the poor
        and the oppressed,
      the homeless and the refugee,
      the hopeless and the weak.
  When I care for those in need,
    I witness that Christ lives in me.
  When I challenge the rulers of the people
      to care for the helpless,
    I witness that the living Christ cares
      about those who hurt.

How shall I tell this government of the resurrection?
  Here in Jerusalem we are under Roman rule,
    and much of our taxes go to Rome's
      far-flung armies.

22

The wheat of Galilee,
    sheep from the hills of Bethlehem,
    olive oil from the Mount of Olives,
        all go to feed the Roman garrisons,
            while the poor of Jerusalem beg.

Jesus, when we walked with him,
    wept over every injustice:
spoke to Samaritans,
    whom most people despised,
forgave sinners,
confronted the political authorities,
shook his head at the emptiness
    of those who made money their god.
And Jesus still lives!
I must witness that the risen Christ —
        living in me —
    loves other races and nations,
    offers new life,
    new hope,
        not only to the poor
            but also to the rich,
        not only to the weak
            but also to the high-placed and powerful,
        if only they will take him to their hearts.
The risen Christ speaks to the ill,
    that God cares,
        that he is the great Physician.
He reaches out through us to the lonely:
    that he is present,
        that he will be with them forever.

When I face death, may I do so
    as a witness to the resurrection.
My Lord was crucified for me —
    humiliated, tortured, slain.

If I am faithful to him,
    will I also be persecuted?
If I approach death now, in my prime,
    let it be with confidence in God
        and the assurance I live
            by the resurrection of Christ.
And if I live,
    and the time comes when I have used up
        my span of years,
    God grant me confidence
        that the living Christ is with me,
        so that I shall live and die
            a witness to the resurrection.

Brothers, sisters,
    we gathered here in Jerusalem are 120 believers,
        plus a few more up in Galilee,
    in our nation of four million souls.
When we leave this room,
    you may be the only Christian in your village —
        in your marketplace —
            in your caravan.
And beyond our nation is Samaria —
    and Greece and Rome —
        and the whole world.
How shall we ever start this task?
But if we do not start,
    how shall it ever be done?

Christ our Lord lives,
    and by the joy of his resurrection
        we have joy day to day
        and day to day courage
        and day to day power.
    Joy — courage — power
        to bear witness to the resurrection.
        What else could we want? The Lord is risen indeed!

Which, Simon:
A Boat Or A Life?

Every child in church school knows of Jesus' call to Simon and Andrew, James and John to become "fishers of men." They left everything to follow him. What we do not know is the effect of this call on their families and their friends; likewise we do not know how they disposed of their property, nor do we know whether they ever looked back.

* * *

Standin' on the shore I was,
 knee-deep in the water,
 cleanin' my net,
  when I heard Simon shout.
Zebedee's sons had their boat still in the water,
 and they went to help him pull his net.
It tossed and flipped with more fish
 than I'd ever seen in one catch in all my life.
They all came to shore,

both boats so loaded they were about to sink.
Simon stepped out,
    pulled his boat up,
        and called me over.
"Jacob," he said,
    "we've been friends for many a year.
    Here."
He took my hand and set it on his boat;
    then he laid his big hand on my shoulder.
"Here, Jacob, this is yours."

"Why, Simon, why?" I asked him.
He looked at the boat,
    well-worn, sturdy like himself,
        and at the heap of fish, shinin' in the sun.
"It's yours," he said.
    "I won't need it anymore.
The Master has called me,
    and I'm going to follow him."
He turned and walked away,
    he and his brother Andrew,
        James and John,
            all walking with that man Jesus.

I didn't know what to do:
    sell the fish for him,
        or what?
But then I went to his house that night.
    It was crowded;
        I couldn't even shove my way in.
Jesus sat inside, with people packed around him,
    listening, looking for help,
        begging to be healed.
Dozens squeezed together at the doorway,
    trying to catch a word.
I called for Simon, and he pushed his way out.
"What's happening, Simon?

What did you mean with your boat this morning?
What's it all about?"

He looked at me with that way of his,
        gruff and friendly at the same time,
    and he said,
        "I'm a new man now, Jacob,
            a new man with a new calling.
        It started with my brother Andrew,
            when he went to see John the Baptist.
        He heard John and felt his power.
        Could John be the Messiah?
            But John said, 'No.'
    Then Jesus came up,
        and John the Baptist said,
            'Look! Here is the lamb of God,
                who takes away the sin of the world!
            I only baptize with water;
                he's the one who baptizes
                    with the Holy Spirit and with fire.
                This is the son of God.
            There's your answer,' John told Andrew.
            'He's the Messiah.
            Follow him!'

"Andrew came to me —
    we've always done things together —
and he said to me,
    'We've found the Messiah!'
I went with him to Jesus,
    and I believed.
I can't explain it,
    but he's made me feel like a new person,
    a better person — somehow, God's person.

"Well," Simon went on,
    "that was a couple of months ago,

27

and I didn't see Jesus again until last week,
   here in Capernaum.
Yesterday he healed a man in the synagogue —
   you must have heard about it.
When the service was over,
   I begged him to come to my house.
   My wife's mother was sick in bed,
   and we were worried.
He just told the fever to leave her,
   and she was well.
We couldn't keep her in bed;
   she got up and fixed dinner.

"You saw what happened this morning.
   We had fished all night
   and didn't have one fish for breakfast.
I was washing my net,
   about to go home empty-handed,
     when Jesus came along with a crowd.
'Let me have your boat, Simon,' he asked.
He climbed in, and I shoved out a little way,
   so that everyone could see him and hear him.
And what he said was true.
   He spoke to me as the very word of God.

"After he talked to the crowd, he said to me,
   'Simon, go out where it's deep
   and let down your net.'
'It's no use,' I told him.
   'We fished all night,
   and we know there ain't no fish here.'
But I wanted to please him,
   and, well, you saw what happened.
   We couldn't lift the net, it was so full.
   I don't know what to make of it.
Then he said, 'Simon, don't be afraid.
   Come, follow me;
     I'll make you a fisher of men.'

"That was that.
   I gave you the boat, Jacob.
   Jesus called; I follow.
   I can't do anything else.
I've thought of it all day.
   He heals when the doctors can't.
      He teaches what the rabbis don't know.
         He puts the fish in a fisherman's net.
He's just who John the Baptist said he is:
   the Messiah,
      the son of God.
Keep the boat, old friend;
   I'm going with Jesus."

So Simon went —
   walked off, left kinfolk, house, boat, everything —
   for Jesus.
They passed by here off and on, every few weeks:
   Simon and Andrew with Jesus,
      James and John,
         eight or ten others.
Then the last time they came by
   on the way to Jerusalem,
      I could see Simon was upset.
"Simon," I said,
   "We've fished this sea together,
      by moonlight, starlight, sunset, and dawn;
   we've pulled nets together in calm waters
      and storms as bad as a man can stand.
   Simon, I've never seen you so troubled before."

"Jacob," he said, "I've been to strange places.
   Jesus took us up to the top of Mt. Hermon.
   There he began to shine — white —
      like an angel.
   And two men were there —
      don't call me crazy —

29

one was Moses;
the other was Elijah.
As I live, they were there!
They talked with him.
A voice came out of the cloud,
and they were gone.
When we came down,
he said we were going to Jerusalem,
and he would be killed.
I don't know what's happening ...
but I must follow.
There is nothing in this world I can do
but follow him.''

The next morning they were gone.
Then families who had gone to Jerusalem
for the Passover came back with the news:
Jesus had been crucified;
Simon and the others had scattered.
I was sorry to hear it.
Jesus was a good man.
He helped a lot of folks here:
healed them, fed them, comforted them.
We'll miss him.
And I was sorry for Simon and the others:
they'd left everything to follow Jesus,
and now it was all over.

It was six weeks before I saw Simon again,
and he was a different man.
He came back burstin' at the seams with his story:
that Jesus was alive,
that he and the others had seen Jesus,
several times,
risen from the dead.
But at the same time he was troubled, restless.
One minute he was confident,

wanting to tell everyone that Jesus was alive;
the next minute he was ready to give up.

"What is it, Simon?
    What's bothering you?"
His shoulders slumped.
    "I've failed, Jacob, I've failed.
        Jesus is alive,
        and I want to tell the whole world,
            but I am a failure.
    When he was arrested,
        I ran.
    When he was on trial,
        I swore I didn't even know him."
He turned his head,
        and I heard him sob.
            Simon was a brokenhearted man.

The next morning he was a different person,
        erect, confident, joyful.
    "Shalom, Simon," I greeted him.
        "You look like a fine sunny morning."
    "Shalom, Jacob, it is a fine morning,"
        he answered, and he told me the story.
    "You saw how upset I was last night.
    I was restless, so six of us went fishing.
    We worked all night and didn't have a minnow.
    Then a man stood on the shore
        and told us where to throw the net.
    It was like that first catch, three years ago:
        so many fish the net was breaking.
    I knew at once it had to be Jesus.
    We came ashore,
        and he had a fire ready,
            with bread and fish.
    Then he looked at me.
        'Simon, son of Jonah,

do you love me?'
'Yes.'
'Feed my lambs, tend my sheep.'
Three times he asked me —
　　like the three times I denied him —
　　　　and he told me to care for his lambs.
He trusted me —
　　trusted me again, after my failure.
He's forgiven me —
　　forgiven me —
　　　　and trusted me with his people.
I know he still loves me,
　　and I love him."

Then, at last, I began to understand Simon:
　　why he'd given me his boat —
　　　　why he'd followed Jesus —
　　　　　　and why he would follow Jesus
　　　　　　　　to the end of the world.

Simon had found one person
　　who meant more than a house, a boat, and nets —
and, in the long run,
　　more than a thriving business,
　　　　a house on two acres,
　　　　　　and a new Pontiac.

Simon had found one person who means more than
　　Governor Pontius Pilate or King Herod,
　　　　more than the rituals of the Temple
　　　　　　and the approval of the Pharisees
and, in the long run,
　　more than public opinion polls
　　　　or newspaper headlines
　　　　or golf on Sunday mornings
　　　　or even more than next year's World Series.

Simon had found life!
   He had found the one person who is life,
      life itself —
      life that is a part of being myself and yourself,
      life that is a part of being a family,
         part of friendship,
      life that makes the rest of life worth living.

Yes, Simon, at last I understand.
   This is why you did it.
   The choice was between a boat or a life,
      and you chose life.

John 19:38-42

Joseph Of Arimathea: Closet Christian

In Glastonbury, England, some curious hawthorn bushes flower twice a year. They are reported to be a variety not native to England but related to those of the eastern Mediterranean, and there is a legend about them. William of Malmsbury, about the year 1135, recorded the legend that Joseph of Arimathea left Jerusalem and went to southern France. From there, in 63 A.D., he went to Britain and founded the first Christian settlement in England at the site of present-day Glastonbury. He took with him his walking staff, cut from his garden in Jerusalem. When he stuck the staff into the ground in England, it rooted, becoming the Glastonbury thorn.

All four Gospels mention one event in the life of Joseph of Arimathea; each adds some of the details. But Joseph must have a story of his own.

* * *

Why am I here on your shore,
my sandals well-worn,

35

this staff in my hand?
Briefly, in the name of Jesus
I have lost everything I had,
and by the love of Jesus I have gained far more.

Let me begin.
I am a Hebrew,
born in Arimathea in the province of Judea.
I inherited large farms,
and by hard work I increased my wealth.
Yet I knew also that life is more
than heaping up wheat and oil and wine or gold.
From my youth I have loved the one almighty God,
Creator of all things,
God of Israel and God of my Fathers.
In that love for God, I became a Pharisee,
the strictest sect of our people,
trying to keep perfectly all the law of God.
For my religious zeal,
as well as my wealth and social status,
I was chosen to be a member of the Sanhedrin,
the council of elders and high priests
that ruled the Temple
and the religious life of my people.

It was a good life:
my position on the council brought prestige
and greater business opportunities.
As a ruler in the Temple,
I grew in my worship of God.
Still, life was not quite full;
I had a hunger for something more.
Then I met Jesus,
and my world turned upside down.

The council heard that a man named Jesus
was going from town to town,

teaching new ideas and drawing huge crowds.
Naturally we were apprehensive,
    for he had no training from the rabbis;
    there was no telling what dreadful errors
        he could introduce.
It was reported that he did great miracles of healing;
    we were skeptical;
    this must be nonsense from the mob.
Then Jesus came to Jerusalem,
    teaching in the Temple courtyard,
        healing in the streets.
When he healed a paralyzed man,
    he threw our council into consternation.
There was no doubt:
    the man had been paralyzed for years,
        and he was completely healed;
    but Jesus had done this on the Sabbath day,
        which is for worship only.
Healing was good;
breaking the Sabbath was evil;
    was this Jesus from God or from the Devil?
I had to hear Jesus for myself.
    Each time I listened,
        my soul stirred within me.
His words held me, convinced me,
    fed the long-time hunger in my life.
He stood in the Temple and cried out,
    "Let anyone who is thirsty come to me,
        and let the one who believes in me drink.
    As the scripture has said,
    'Out of the believer's heart shall flow rivers
        of living water.' "
I felt my thirst;
    within my heart I believed
        and drank of his truth,
            and my thirst was satisfied.

I knew in my inmost being he was the Messiah,
   the Holy One sent by God,
     the living Son of God.
What did I do?
   What did I say?
   Nothing.
     Nothing.

Most of the council was against Jesus,
   and they sent temple police to arrest him.
The police returned empty-handed, saying,
   "Never has anyone spoken like this!"
Leaders of the council berated Jesus
   without hearing him.
Nicodemus,
   an older, well-respected member,
   had the courage to defend him indirectly,
   asking,
     "Our law does not judge people
     without first giving them a hearing
     to find out what they are doing, does it?"
The council leaders then vented their scorn
   on Nicodemus.
What did I do?
   What did I say?
   Nothing.
I was respected by the council,
   but so was Nicodemus.
   If they brushed him aside,
     they would do the same to me.
   There were good men on the council,
     but the leaders were political appointees,
     concerned only for their power,
     and they had set their minds against Jesus.
My judgment was influential,
   but I knew in advance I would be outvoted.

I justified my silence by thinking,
    "Perhaps Jesus will need more help later,
    but if I join Nicodemus now,
        I will lose the power to influence events
            another time."
    Again, I was silent.

For two years I carried my faith in my bosom;
    it grew stronger each time I heard Jesus.
Then came the crisis.
Each spring our people celebrate the Passover,
    a great holy festival.
    I had been out in the country for several days,
        talking to my farm managers
        and arranging for the spring work.
    Then I rushed back to Jerusalem for the Passover,
        hoping that Jesus would be there
        and I would see him again.

When I arrived in the city,
    I learned the dreadful news.
    The council had arrested Jesus,
        condemned him in a hurried nighttime trial,
            and turned him over to the Romans
                on false charges;
        he was now being nailed to a cross,
            the terrible Roman execution.
Waves of guilt and shame poured over me.
    Why hadn't I spoken up for him before?
    Why had I been away this week?
    Why hadn't I been at the council to defend him?
    What could I do?
    Was there nothing I could do now?

I went to the place of execution,
    a hill near the city,

My heart sank at the agony,
   the brutality.
To see a man of God,
   one who was more than man,
   one who was God come for us in human flesh:
   to see this one who had spoken such truth
      and done so much good,
   to see him mocked and tortured
      was more than I could bear.

I searched for Nicodemus,
   and I found him at the edge of the crowd.
Since his defense of Jesus,
   we had spoken many times,
      and we had shared in secret
         our faith in Jesus the Messiah.
He told me the council had met at night,
   an illegal time,
   and he had not been invited.
Did they suspect I was a believer?
   Was that why they had not called me in
      from the country?

The sky grew black,
   the earth shook,
      and we knew Jesus was dead.
Roman soldiers trembled,
   and we heard them say,
      "Truly this man was God's Son!"

What could we do?
It was too late to save Jesus' life.
   But must he hang there on the cross for days?
   It is a disgrace in Israel
      for a body to remain unburied,
         doubly a disgrace when it is a man of God.

Yet by Roman law,
    the body of an executed criminal
    belonged to the government;
    no one dared to touch it
      without the governor's permission.
"I will go to the governor," I told Nicodemus.
    "I know him; maybe he will give permission
    for a decent burial."
I knew the cost:
    I might risk the Governor's anger;
    I would certainly face retaliation
      from the leaders of the council.

Why did I do it?
    It was an act of love
      for the teacher who taught such love.
    It was an act of respect
      to one who treated all persons with respect.
    It was an act of despair and guilt,
      for my Lord was dead,
        and I had failed to help him
          when he was in need.
Why did I do it?
    There were deeper reasons.
Once Jesus had said to me,
    "Some day, Joseph,
      you must declare yourself.
    You must be for me or against me."
Now the day had come.
Jesus' death did for me
    what even his life had not done.
The hesitation, the concealment, had to go.
I must put aside my fear
    and show my faith.
Why did I do it?
    I later learned Jesus had told his inner circle,

"I, when I am lifted up from the earth,
    will draw all people to myself."
Already the power of his cross
    was turning this coward
        into the man you see now:
        a man who took an irreversible step
        for Jesus the Christ.

Pilate gave his permission.
Then Nicodemus and I had to move quickly.
    It was late in the day,
        and under Jewish law the burial
            must be finished before sundown
            and the start of the holy Passover.
    We had one big advantage.
        I owned a new tomb,
            which I had prepared for myself and my family.
        It was dug in the face of a rock cliff,
            quite near the place of the crucifixion.
    While our servants carried the body of Jesus
        to my tomb,
    Nicodemus bought spices to anoint the body.
    We buried Jesus,
        and the servants rolled a heavy stone
            over the entrance to the tomb.

Nicodemus and I went to our homes,
        tired,
            brokenhearted.
    We both knew we had sacrificed
        our positions on the council,
            our public respect,
                probably our wealth,
                    possibly even our lives.
    Yet we had to do what we had done,
        and we knew it was right.
It was a time of sorrow.

42

On the third day,
life changed completely!
His disciples brought the joyful news.
Jesus had risen from the dead!
Jesus was alive!
They had seen him alive!
He had met them,
talked with them,
eaten with them.
Jesus was alive!
Our faith was vindicated,
our hopes were renewed,
Jesus was alive!

For several weeks the risen Jesus met with us.
He taught us the meaning of his coming
and his death.
In his death and rising again,
Jesus had brought us forgiveness and new life.
He had fulfilled God's ancient promises to our people,
giving us a new covenant
open to all nations of the world.
Then God sent his Holy Spirit upon us
with great power.
In that power we have gone out
telling of new life by faith in Jesus the Christ.
In every land,
to the north and to the south,
to the east and to the west,
men and women beyond counting
have heard this good news,
received it in their hearts,
rejoiced in this new life
by faith in Jesus Christ.

Friends, I have travelled many miles
by land and by sea
to bring this message to your shore.

Jesus is alive!
Jesus is Lord, Son of God, Savior, Redeemer;
    and Jesus offers the gift of life,
    life that is full and rich,
    life that is eternal,
    love that drives out fear,
    the transforming, empowering,
        all-embracing love of our gracious God.

Good people of this new land, that is my story.
Once I kept my faith in a closet,
        safely hidden away.
    I heard people complain of the emptiness of life,
        and I failed to tell them of the Savior
            who could fill the voids of their souls.
    I knew people who were troubled or depressed,
        and I did not spend the time
            to take them to Jesus who could lift them up;
        I did not show them the greater joy
            of life in Christ.
    I saw people throw their entire enthusiasm
            into business or politics or sports or travel,
            leaving little place in their lives for God,
        and I did not show them the greater joy
            and greater enthusiasm of life in Christ.
Friends, I came out of that closet,
    I did not hold back my tomb,
        or my reputation,
        or my safety.
    I gave myself to Jesus Christ,
        and he has given Himself to me.
    I have left behind me all that I had,
        but I bring to you that which is worth far more.
    I bring the good news of the love of God,
        of salvation offered freely
            to all who trust in Jesus as God's Son.
    I bring to you God's gifts
        of life and love and joy and peace. Amen.

Luke 10:38-42
John 12:1-10

Mary of Bethany:
My Radical Sister

"Martha, your work must be punished and counted as naught . . . I will have no work but the work of Mary; that is the faith that you have in the Word."

(Martin Luther)

Medieval legends about Mary of Bethany often confused her with Mary Magdalene; some credited her with a ministry in France. From Luther to the present, many commentators have praised Mary as the more spiritual of the two sisters. Because she sat at Jesus' feet and listened, she was often praised as the model of the demure, submissive Christian woman. Yet in the mores of her patriarchal age, she was hardly demure — anything but!

*   *   *

My sister Mary?
    Some people are still wagging their tongues;

45

they say she has disgraced our village
	and shamed our family.
I was shocked, too,
	and I'm still a little puzzled,
	but I love her,
		and I am very proud of her.

Mary was always my little sister:
	quiet, while I was more active;
	people saw me as the leader.
Now Mary is the bold one,
	and I feel like I am the little sister,
		tagging along after her.
It's as if she has broken down the walls
	that keep us women in a second place,
		and I don't know where it's going to lead.

I was always more outspoken;
	some even called me bossy.
If a family in town was sick,
	or a woman had a new baby,
	I was the one who got the women together,
		planned who would get the meals,
		told everyone what to do.
Mary always did her share with the others,
	but she left the talking to me.

Everything changed when Jesus came through town.
	We had all heard him before:
	Mary, our brother Lazarus, and I.
He spoke to us so directly, so clearly,
	that in him we felt the love of God.
I urged him to come to my house for dinner.
His whole band was with him,
	so there would be a lot of work;
	but I knew Mary would help me,
		as she always does.
		She's a good cook and a hard worker.

There was so much to do all at once:
    vegetables in the pot,
        meat to turn on the fire,
            bread to bake —
              and where was Mary?
    Had she gone to get something?
    Then I saw her in the room with the men,
        sitting at Jesus' feet,
           listening!
I couldn't believe it!
    Just when I needed her most!
    And with the men!
It shocked everyone!
    Women don't study with a rabbi.
    Women don't sit with men in the synagogue —
        we sit in the balcony or behind a screen.
    Men don't allow women to study!
    But there she was,
        breaking all the rules that said "men only,"
        not even noticing the dark frowns
            of the elders of the synagogue,
        eyes and ears only for Jesus.

It was too much!
    I was frantic,
        with dinner for Jesus and his 12 disciples
            and our brother and a dozen others —
        and my best helper sat down.
    My little sister was shocking the town
        and disgracing the family,
        and my brother didn't say a word to stop her.
I guess I lost my temper,
    and I wasn't the perfect hostess.
    I blurted out to Jesus,
        "Lord, don't you care that my sister has left me
            to do all the work by myself?
        Tell her then to help me."

Jesus wasn't upset by my outburst,
    and he wasn't shocked by Mary's behavior.
  He spoke to me calmly, soothingly,
    "Martha, Martha, you are worried and distracted
      by many things;
    there is need of only one thing.
    Mary has chosen the better part,
      which will not be taken away from her."
  He accepted Mary,
    sitting there with the men,
      as if women have a right to learn,
      as if women are equal to men.
  It was as if Mary had smashed a hole through the wall —
    the wall that kept us confined to kitchen and children
    and balcony.

Later I remembered that Joanna and Mary Magdalene
    and Susanna and others travelled with Jesus,
    as students travel with a rabbi.
  Jesus treated them as equals,
    and he taught them as he taught the men.
  Could he even have meant that women
    can become rabbis too?

Then came that terrible time when our brother died.
  Lazarus was sick.
  Mary and I were both worried, deeply worried;
    we'd never seen him so ill before.
  We thought, "If only Jesus were here.
    He has healed so many,
      and we know he loves Lazarus."
  We had heard he was beyond the Jordan,
    and our cousin offered to find him.

The next day, Lazarus died.
Mary and I were heartbroken.
  We knew in our heads that Jesus
    could not have come in time;
    it's a two-day journey each way.

Still, we felt in our hearts some resentment
    that Jesus had not been here
        when we most needed him.

Four days later, Mary and I were in the house,
    receiving condolences,
    when someone shouted, "Jesus is coming."
I dashed out, and —
    me and my big mouth —
    I met him with words that were half accusation,
        half faith.
    "Lord, if you had been here,
        my brother would not have died.
    But even now I know that God will give you
        whatever you ask of him."
Jesus ignored my slap in the face,
    and he answered quietly, confidently,
    "Your brother will rise again."

I didn't grasp his full meaning.
    I knew some of the rabbis spoke of a resurrection,
        but they never explained it very well.
    Jesus answered with assurance,
        and he made it very personal.
    "I am the resurrection and the life.
        Those who believe in me,
            even though they die,
                will live ...
    Do you believe this?"

A new understanding flooded my soul,
    and for the first time I began to realize
        why Mary sat at Jesus' feet,
            spellbound, transformed.
    I answered,
            and God must have given me the words,
        "Yes, Lord, I believe that you are the Messiah,
            the Son of God."

I ran to call Mary,
    and she greeted Jesus as I had,
        but in her the words were full-formed faith,
    "Lord, if you had been here,
        my brother would not have died."
You know the rest.
    Even Jesus' enemies know it and cannot deny it.
Jesus went to the tomb,
    told the men to move away the stone,
        prayed to God, and called,
            "Lazarus, come out!"
My brother —
    by then he had been in the tomb four days —
        walked out, alive.

Mary and I were overwhelmed with love for Jesus
        and thanksgiving for our brother's return,
    but it was Mary who showed that love
        in a new and spectacular way.
About six months later,
    Jesus came to Bethany on his way to Jerusalem
        for the Passover.
We all had dinner for him in Simon's house;
    my house wasn't large enough.
The husbands were all at table;
    I was helping the other women serve the meal.
We were so busy
    I didn't notice Mary had disappeared.

Mary returned, but not to help with the food.
    She slipped in where Jesus was reclining with the men,
        poured a whole flask of ointment on his feet,
            and began to wipe his feet with her hair.
I gasped!
    One puts two or three drops of ointment
        on the forehead of an honored guest;
    Mary poured a whole pound on Jesus' feet.

The entire house, the entire neighborhood,
was filled with the perfume.
The guests were shocked!
I covered my face with my hands!
Not even a slave
would wipe a man's feet with her hair,
and this was no ordinary man;
he was a rabbi.
A rabbi does not touch any woman in public,
not even his own wife.
Some of our neighbors shrank away from Mary.
They began to mutter.
It was a disgrace!
It was indecent!
She should be put out of the synagogue!
Jesus' reply puzzled us all.
"Leave her alone.
She bought it so that she might keep it
for the day of my burial."

I didn't understand at all until Jesus had risen.
First, though, there was that dreadful time
when we heard Jesus had been arrested,
tried,
crucified.
We were crushed.
Lazarus, Mary, all his friends,
we were crushed.
How could it be?
He who was all goodness,
he who said he was life itself,
how could he be dead?

On Monday his disciples brought the news:
Jesus was alive!
Mary Magdalene had seen him in the morning.
Others had seen him in the afternoon.

He had been with the whole group in the evening.
He had risen!
He was alive!

Then I began to realize what Mary had done.
    The disciples had told us of Jesus' strange words,
        that in Jerusalem he would be betrayed,
            be killed,
                and rise again.
    The men didn't know what he meant.
Mary alone,
    by some intuition,
    had understood what none of the men had understood;
    she had done what none of the men had dared to do.

I wonder, though, at what Jesus said about Mary.
    "Truly I tell you,
        wherever this good news is proclaimed
            in the whole world,
        what she has done will be told in remembrance of her."
    How far will this go?
        Will it spread to other lands?
        Did Jesus mean that men will hear of Mary
            and accept her thoughts and her actions
            as he accepted them?
    And did he mean that women,
        sometime in the future,
        will remember that Mary had the courage
        to break through the walls
            that kept her in the kitchen,
            in the nursery,
            in the balcony?
    Will Jesus' approval of Mary lead other women —
            and men —
        to sweep away those barriers
        and accept each other as equals
            in the service of the Gospel?

Sometimes I chuckle when I remember
what people used to say about Mary:
she was the quiet one, so demure.
She was quiet, all right,
but she set the whole town buzzing
without saying a word.
Yet what of the future?
Will her actions —
and Jesus' approval —
lead other women to speak up,
use their abilities,
and take the lead in expressing their faith?

Romans 1:1, 7, 15-16; 3:23;
5:1, 6-11; 8:1; 16:1-2

God's Great
Trumpet Call

In a house in ancient Corinth, eight men and a woman sit
on low cushions, all their attention riveted on a ninth man,
unquestionably the leader, pacing the floor, thinking, firing
questions, holding them all with his intensity.

*   *   *

So, Phoebe, you are going to Rome.
How I long to be on the same ship —
embrace in a holy embrace
the brothers and sisters there —
so many I have worked and travelled with.
Some are my children,
by the grace of God born in Christ by faith,
through me and the gospel I teach.
So many others I have heard of,
as if I know them and they know me.
I long to see them all

and then go on to Spain,
    preach Jesus Christ
      to that far-off end of the world.
In the providence of God, I hope to do that next,
    but first I go to Jerusalem.

Phoebe, faithful deacon of the church,
    go to Rome with our blessing.
  Take with you our love,
    the love of all of us to all the church.
  I will send with you a letter:
    my friends will surely care for you.
Tertius, good friend,
    thank you for bringing your inkpot.
  Let us start.
  "Paul, a servant of Jesus Christ,
    called to be an apostle,
      set apart for the gospel of God,
    to all God's beloved in Rome,
      who are called to be saints:
    Grace to you and peace from God our Father
    and the Lord Jesus Christ."

What shall I say to God's household at Rome?
  Gaius, what do they need?
  Quartus, what will help them live Jesus Christ
    in that great city?
  Rome is power.
    Rome is the world power.
    Rome lives by power,
      respects power,
        worships power.
  But we live by another power,
    a greater power,
      a higher power.
  Write this,
  "I am not ashamed of the gospel;

it is the power of God for salvation
to everyone who has faith,
to the Jew first and also to the Greek.''
What is the central fact of daily life?
I've just said it:
the gospel —
the good news
the power of God for salvation —
in Rome —
and when I go to Spain,
God's power will be the good news
of salvation in Christ Jesus.

But now I am writing to Rome.
What are their needs?
Their doubts?
Their fears?
Erastus, as city treasurer,
you've been there on business.
You've told me their sins are those
I've found everywhere:
greed, envy, jealousy, materialism, lust —
and Rome's cruelty.
Yes, I like your illustration.
Rome, you say, sits on a three-legged stool:
the military — slavery — and commerce.
She trusts in military might,
maintaining a worldwide army
even if the cost bankrupts society.
Slaves have replaced freeborn farmers,
who drift to the city,
landless and unemployed.
Food has to be imported to feed the city,
and Caesar taxes all the commerce:
he makes his friends wealthy
and the rest of the empire poor.

And worse, they don't care.
　　Of all the sins they are surrounded by,
　　　　that may be the worst,
　　　　　　those who do not care.
　　They sink into their seats at the Colosseum
　　　　and the shows go by:
　　　　　　chariot races,
　　　　　　then gladiators thumping
　　　　　　　　and beating one another for pay,
　　　　　　then — as if one flicked a switch —
　　　　　　　　soldiers chasing criminals
　　　　　　　　　　and hacking them to pieces.
When one tires of the violence,
　　　　leave the Colosseum and go to the theatre.
　　The first play makes a mockery,
　　　　a buffoonery, of sex:
　　　　the gift of God,
　　　　　　created as a holy fire
　　　　　　　　within the joys of marriage,
　　　　　　　　turned into a bawdy joke.
　　Or — a flip of a switch —
　　　　the next play with sex turned to violence,
　　　　　　sex perverted and depraved.
This must break the heart of every Christian
　　　　in that vast city:
　　the crowds,
　　　　the crowds of those who do not care —
　　　　　　not for the poor,
　　　　　　not for God,
　　　　　　not for Christ,
　　　　　　not for their own souls,
　　　　　　not for anyone else —
　　　　　　　　they don't care.

Does God care?
Yes. God cares.

When all have sinned
    and fallen short of the glory of God,
        God still cares.
He forgives those who come to him in faith.
He counts their faith, their trust in him
    as righteousness.
Take your pen, Tertius, and tell them this,
    "Therefore, since we are justified by faith
        we have peace with God
        through our Lord Jesus Christ.
For while we were still weak,
    at the right time Christ died for the ungodly.
Indeed, rarely will anyone die
    for a righteous person —
        though perhaps for a good person
            someone might actually dare to die.
But God proves his love for us
    in that while we were still sinners
        Christ died for us.
Much more surely then,
    now that we have been justified by his blood,
        will we be saved through him
            from the wrath of God.
For if while we were enemies,
    we were reconciled to God
        through the death of his Son,
    much more surely,
        having been reconciled,
        will we be saved by his life.
But more than that,
    We even boast in God
        through our Lord Jesus Christ,
        through whom we have now
            received reconciliation."
Forgiven —
    loved by God —
        reconciled to God —
            declared righteous —

so completely forgiven that God sees us
        as if we had never sinned.
This is the act of God —
        the gracious love of God —
                the wonderful free gift of God in Jesus Christ.

Then what do we do about it?
        How do we live this full salvation?
        Can the gospel work in the capital of the Empire?
Our friends at Rome wrestle with the daily struggle
        of the Christian life:
        — to keep a marriage whole
                and raise up children in a city
                        where greed and promiscuity
                                are constantly paraded before their eyes.
        — to conduct one's business
                with an integrity that shows
                        that one belongs to Jesus Christ.
        — to worship in a way
                that shares the grace of Christ.
If I were there,
        how could I show that vast secular city
                what it means to be a new person in Christ?
        The daily struggle
        and when one falls short —
                for all of us —
                Timothy and Luke, my companions,
                and you, Gaius, my host,
                and I, Paul,
                all have times when we feel our guilt —
                        and then begin to doubt.
If my salvation is real,
        then why do I still envy —
                lose my temper —
                        have hurt feelings?
How many of us can square our shoulders
        and say,
                "I have measured up

to my own highest expectations?"
Fear and guilt make us start to doubt our faith.

How hard it must be there in Rome!
The sins on which the city is built
hammer at the doors,
demanding entrance into a person's life:
militarism —
racial pride —
an unjust economic system —
the brutalizing spectacles of violence —
permissive sex —
greed —
all these try to force their way
into a Christian's life.
And the Christian asks,
"Is faith enough?
Can God really forgive?"
And God's answer is a thundering "Yes!"
God does not wait to show his love.
While we were still sinners Christ died for us.
We are saved by him from the wrath of God.
It's God's gift —
full, free, unconditional gift!

Write this to the believers at Rome:
when they struggle with guilt,
"The conclusion of the matter is this.
There is no condemnation —
no blame, no judgment, no penalty —
for those who are in Christ Jesus,
because in Christ Jesus
the life-giving law of the Spirit
has set you free from the law of sin and death."
That is the gospel.
That is the good news.
No penalty can hang over your head.
In Christ you are forgiven.

Listen.
Listen with the ears of your mind.
    Do you hear the blowing of a trumpet —
        the shophar —
        the long trumpet that the priest blows
            on the day of atonement —
        a sign of repentance —
        of God taking away the sins of the year —
            atoned for, forgiven, remembered no more?

Listen.
Here is a greater trumpet —
        God's great trumpet call.
    In Jesus Christ there is one great eternal
        day of atonement.
    He has lifted away our sins for all time.
    This is God's atonement:
        full salvation in the face of evils,
            both of the flesh and of the world outside.

This is the letter we must send to Rome.
This is the good news!
    By the power of God we are forgiven,
        we are free,
            we have the grace of God.
    This is what we must tell them:
        the assurance that they belong to Christ,
        and nothing shall separate them from his love.
        — When we have wrestled with sin,
            and turned to God —
            there is no condemnation.
        — When we have wrestled with ourselves —
            there is the grace of God.
        — When we have wept and cried and repented
            about our economic evils —
            there is no condemnation.

— When we have anguished over military power,
　　the offer is true to every soldier —
　　　every centurion —
　　the offer is true to the emperor himself
　　　if he will only listen —
　　in Christ there is no condemnation.
— When we have spoken out
　　about the brutality of the gladiators
　　　and the heedlessness of the mobs
　　　　in the street,
　　Christ offers still his gospel —
　　　in Christ there is no condemnation.
— When we have struggled
　　with the doubts of Christians —
　　the fears of church members —
　　and the sins of believers,
　　the answer of God is still his grace —
　　there is no condemnation.

Blow the long shophar for God's day of atonement!
　Sound the great trumpet call of God's forgiveness!
　There is now no condemnation
　　for those who are in Christ Jesus!

Luke 15:4-7

Mark: A
Second Chance

---

*Place yourself, for a moment, in ancient Rome: not in the
Forum or a palace or the Colosseum — that hasn't yet been
built — but in a little house on a side street. Before you sits
an older man, his hair white, his shoulders bent by years of
hard work, but his manner confident and his voice strong.*

* * *

Mark?
   I don't know what I'd do without him.
      He's as fine a young man as they come.
   Hah! Did I call him a young man?
   He's as much a young man
      as I am still a fisherman —
      and I haven't pulled a net these thirty years.
   "Peter the Fisherman,"
      that's how some still remember me.
         "Peter, the Old Fisherman."

65

And I guess I remember Mark as I first met him —
    a youth —
    and forget he's mature now.
  But I can't forget all he's done
      in the service of Christ.
Yes, Mark had his failings.
  He was with us in the garden
    the night Jesus was arrested —
      and he ran —
        so did we all.
  A soldier grabbed him by the robe
    and he wiggled out —
      ran away naked.
  We were all scared that night —
    and crushed the next day.
  We didn't know Jesus would rise from the dead,
    and that would make all the difference
      in the world.

Mark and his mother knew the risen Christ.
  When Herod threw me into jail,
    it was in Mark's mother's house
      the church gathered to pray for me.
  Anyway, we all knew Mark,
    and watched him grow
    and rejoiced with him in the love of Christ.

Mark's first call to service became his big failure.
  When Paul and Barnabas were set apart
    for their first big missionary trip,
    Mark went along to help them.
      Barnabas was Mark's cousin, you know.
  They started in Cyprus,
    the easy part of the trip.
  But when they got to Perga on the mainland,
    Mark left and went home to Jerusalem.

That's when the trip became harder:
opposition,
        driven out of town,
            stoned and left for dead at Lystra;
    Mark missed all that hard part.
Paul and Barnabas felt let down,
    the church felt let down,
        and Mark himself felt let down:
            he knew he was a failure.
Worse yet,
    when Paul and Barnabas planned a second mission,
        Barnabas wanted to take Mark,
            give him a chance to make good.
    Paul absolutely refused.
        Paul said this was no job for a loser, a quitter.
        Mark is useless;
            he showed that the first time.
It got so sharp it split Paul and Barnabas apart:
    two great men who'd held each other up
        all through great dangers, great opposition,
            and they broke over Mark.
Paul found a new companion — Silas —
    and started off on the trip that took the Gospel
        to Macedonia and then to Greece:
            the first teaching of Christ in Europe.

Most Christians agreed with Paul.
    They gave up on Mark as a lost sheep,
        gone on the wrong path,
            and never going to amount to anything.
I can still hear the words of Jesus,
    as clearly as the day when he said them,
    Which one of you, having a hundred sheep and losing one
    of them, does not leave the ninety-nine in the wilderness
    and go after the one that is lost until he finds it? When
    he has found it, he lays it on his shoulders and rejoices.
    And when he comes home, he calls together his friends

and neighbors, saying to them, "Rejoice with me, for I have
found my sheep that was lost." Just so, I tell you, there
will be more joy in heaven over one sinner who repents than
over ninety-nine righteous persons who need no repentance.

Barnabas surely lived those words of Jesus.
    He took Mark with him and went off to Cyprus.
    On that new mission Mark showed his worth
        as a man of God.
Yes, Mark failed on his first big test,
    but Barnabas, bighearted as ever,
        gave him another chance,
            and by the grace of God, Mark made good.
The lost sheep made his way back, rejoicing.
    Barnabas rejoiced,
        the whole church rejoiced,
            and Paul especially rejoiced.

Paul could be firm, very firm,
    when he knew he was right,
    but Paul also knew the redeeming grace of God,
    and how Jesus Christ can change a man.
He never forgot how he himself
    had persecuted Christians
    and how God turned him around.
Paul was my friend;
    he knew how I denied my Lord,
    and he knew how Christ received me back
        and commissioned me for service.
Paul rejoiced in Mark's new growth
    and later took Mark with him on his travels.
When Paul was in prison here in Rome,
    Mark cared for his needs.
Paul wrote to us all that Mark was a comfort to him,
    and he sent Mark on a mission to Colossae
        and to other churches.

Still later, when things when things were hard in prison,
    Paul wrote to Timothy,
      "Get Mark, and bring him with you,
        for he is useful in my ministry."

That's a while ago.
    Mark's older now; I'm much older,
      and Mark is with me here in Rome.
    He's doing something I should have done long ago —
      if I could have.
    He's writing down the story of Jesus.
There's not many of us left,
    we who walked the hills of Galilee with Jesus
      and heard him teach in the villages.
    We are fewer still — I'm almost the only one left —
      who broke bread with him in the upper room,
        ran from the garden,
          huddled together, broken,
            when he was in the tomb,
        and came to life again
          when the risen Christ appeared in the room.
    John's still alive, exiled to Patmos;
    Matthew's in Judea,
    Thomas went to the East,
      and we haven't heard from him.
Someone has to tell the story
    when our generation is gone.
That's why Mark is doing what I cannot do.
    Fisherman I was, and never much of a scribe,
    but in my mind's eye I can see Jesus
      take a lame man by the hand,
    and I can see — just as clearly as it was —
      that lame man stand,
        start to walk,
          then run,
            leap for joy!

And I can hear Jesus teach a crowd
or give a sharp answer to a hypocrite:
it's just as clear in my ears as it was
when he sat in my boat
and taught the people on the shore.
I tell it all to Mark,
just as I saw it, heard it, felt it,
and Mark is writing it down.
I don't think he'll get it all in his scroll.
No papyrus can hold the power of Jesus:
his life;
the health and strength and joy and healings
and bitter tears;
or our absolute amazement when we knew
he had risen;
but Mark will have as much as pen and ink
can carry.

Yes, Mark's as fine as can be,
and the whole church will owe him thanks.
When John and I and all the rest who saw
the risen Christ are gone,
the church will still have the story,
given by the hand of Mark.

Aye. Yet sometimes, when he sits writing, I wonder.
As this church of our Lord Jesus goes on
through the years ahead,
what will happen
to other young Christians who fail?
Will they have a second chance?

In that far-off future day,
will there be a Paul in the church
big enough to say, "I was wrong.
I once judged you a failure,
but now I thank God for what you can become"?

Will there be a Paul with the insight to say,
    "We have all failed God — once — and again —
    and many times.
    But God forgives,
        and by the love of Jesus Christ,
        God makes us new persons, able to start over"?
Will there be a Barnabas in that future church,
        bighearted, a son of encouragement,
    willing to take a chance on a dropout, a failure,
        or the person who doesn't fit in?
    Will there be a Barnabas,
    ready to make some personal effort,
        to give that person a start on the long road back?
How many young men will make a mistake
    and be pushed aside,
        and be afraid to try again,
        or not be trusted,
        not given a chance to prove themselves?
And how many — no matter what they have done —
    will be held up in the arms of a Christian brother
        and given a hug of assurance,
        and grow to take their places in the ranks
            of the faithful servants of our Lord?
How many young women will be put down
        and made to feel ashamed,
    so they feel they are unworthy
        of our Lord's forgiveness,
        and unwelcome in his church;
            then they turn away
                from the love of Christ entirely?
And how many — no matter what they have done —
    will be held in the bosom of their sisters,
    and lifted up in the healing grace of our Lord,
    and become the honored fellow-workers
        among the people of God?

One thing I know.
    Christ our Savior gave me a second chance,
        a third,
           a fourth;
    he took me after I denied him.
He'll do the same for every Mark,
    and Peter,
        and Mary,
        and Paul.
Will they have the faith to turn
    to his restoring love?
Will the Church have the faith,
    the love,
        the courage,
           the vision,
    to accept them,
        encourage them,
          love them,
             rejoice with them,
                and bring them back,
    giving praise and thanks to God?

Acts 19:1−20:1
Ephesians 2:4-6, 8

Demetrius:
Business Is Business

The scroll is worn and old; worms have taken a word here and there; the Greek is the Greek of the marketplace. But let the city official tell his story.

*   *   *

Antiochus,
    Clerk of the Council of the City of Ephesus,
      to His Excellency Junius Silvanus,
        Proconsul of the Province of Asia,
        greetings.

We count ourselves indeed fortunate,
    most noble Junius,
      to welcome you as the new Proconsul
        of our city and our province.
I know you have heard,
    as all the world has heard,

that here is the great temple of Artemis,
    celebrated as one of the wonders of the world.
Here, too, we have a great new theatre,
    with seats for 25,000 people.
Above all, we are the great commercial center
    of Rome's eastern provinces.
To this we all welcome you.

I most humbly regret, your Excellency,
    that I must report to you an incident
        that concerns our temple, our theatre,
            and our commerce.
I beg leave to set straight the facts,
    lest you hear some errant rumor.
There came here three years ago
    some wandering teachers
        who call themselves "the way"
            or "the believers."
They talk of one Jesus,
    whom they call Christ,
    and whom they claim has risen from the dead.
Their leader is a man named Paul,
    of that despised race called Jews,
        who are everywhere clannish,
        will not worship our gods,
        and refuse to bow before the images
            of our illustrious Emperor.
Day and night they persuade the people
    that there is no other god than their god
        who came to them in Jesus,
    and that gods made with hands
        are no gods at all.

They have made many converts.
Paul is reputed to have done miracles of healing.
    Some men who were sorcerers
        have burned their books of magic charms:

74

all gibberish, as you and I know,
    but worth a high price.
What fools would burn their own property?
    But that breaks no laws.

As they grew in numbers, though,
    these people had a regrettable influence
    on our commerce and our prosperity.
The Temple of Artemis draws pilgrims
        from every land,
    and it brings business to all our innkeepers
    and merchants,
    but most especially to the silversmiths
        who sell copies of the shrine
            and the statue of Artemis.
Our Artemis is not your Roman Diana,
    your slender virginal huntress.
Our Artemis is well-rounded,
    a goddess of plenty, many-breasted,
        for she is goddess of fertility
        and nourishes all our people.
Pilgrims pay high prices for her silver shrines,
    to assure the fruitfulness of their fields
    and the fertility of their wives.

So many people have joined the followers of Jesus
    that the stream of pilgrims slowed.
Business slackened,
    and of all merchants,
        the silversmiths were the ones most hurt.
One of the silversmiths, Demetrius,
    took the lead, gathered other craftsmen,
    and stirred them up, saying,
        "Men, you know that we get our wealth
        from this business.
    You also see and hear that not only in Ephesus
        but in almost the whole of Asia

this Paul has persuaded and drawn away
a considerable number of people
by saying that gods made with hands
are not gods.
And there is danger
not only that this trade of ours
may come into disrepute
but also that the temple of the great
goddess Artemis will be scorned,
and she will be deprived of her majesty
that brought all Asia and the world
to worship her."

What a heady brew this was!
The craftsmen were inflamed with religion,
pride in their city,
and business.
"Business is business," cried Demetrius,
"and we cannot have this strange Christian
religion interfering with business."

Most excellent Junius,
be assured that the City Council
had nothing to do with what happened next.
The craftsmen shouted,
"Great is Artemis of the Ephesians!"
In the confusion all sorts of people began to chant,
took hold of two of the Christian teachers,
and dragged them to the theatre.
I learned later that their leader, Paul,
tried to come and to speak,
but his friends stopped him.
Many of the crowd didn't know
why they were there,
but they filled the theatre to overflowing.
For two hours they cried,
"Great is Artemis of the Ephesians."
Anyone who tried to speak was shouted down.

76

Please be assured, most noble Junius,
    that there was no violence, just noise;
        nothing was said against our great Emperor,
    Claudius Caesar,
        just against those few Christians.

When most throats were tired, I spoke.
    "Citizens of Ephesus,
        who is there that does not know
            that the city of Ephesus
            is the temple keeper of the great Artemis
            and of the statue that fell from heaven?
        Since these things cannot be denied,
            you ought to be quiet and do nothing rash.
        You have brought these men here
            who are neither temple robbers
            nor blasphemers of our goddess.
    If therefore Demetrius and the artisans with him
            have a complaint against anyone,
            the courts are open.
        Let them bring charges there,
        for we are in danger of being charged
            with rioting today."
Then I dismissed them.
    That was sufficient.
    They knew the dangers of the charge of rioting:
        bad for business, bad for tourists.
    They went back to their shops,
        and all is quiet.

I trust, if any other report should reach you,
    you will know this was no insurrection,
        but just some noise about that strange religion.
Demetrius is certainly right:
        business is business,
        but he knows now to take an orderly course
            and bring his protest to the officials.

But business is business,
    and when religion interferes with business,
        it is only natural that a businessman
        should seek action.

As for that Paul,
    he shall not cause further trouble here in Ephesus,
    for he has left for Macedonia.
His followers ...

*At this point, wormholes and age have made
the scroll illegible, so we take our leave of the city
clerk.*

We have said good-bye to the city clerk,
    but have we said good-bye to Demetrius
    and his slogan, "Business is business"?
Yes, business is business, but which business?
    Demetrius was in the business of making gods,
    but God is in the business of making you and me.

Demetrius' principle was
    "We get our wealth from this business."
He said nothing of his love for Artemis
    or her love for people,
    nothing of grace,
        forgiveness,
            restoration,
                new life,
            or hope,
    for the cult of Artemis knew nothing of these.

Paul left Ephesus,
    undoubtedly to the relief of Demetrius
    and the city officials,
    but he wrote to remind the believers
        of their business and their true wealth,

God, who is rich in mercy,
out of the great love with which he loved us,
even when we were dead through our trespasses,
made us alive together with Christ —
by grace you have been saved —
and raised us up with him
and seated us with him in the heavenly places
in Christ Jesus ....
For by grace you have been saved through faith,
and this is not your own doing:
it is the gift of God .... (Ephesians 2:4-6, 8)

Cornelius:
Man Of Decision

Jesus instructed his apostles to take the Gospel into all the world. Yet all of the first disciples were Jewish, and the division between Jew and Gentile in the First Century was bitter. Even a moderately religious Jew would never enter a Gentile's house and certainly would not eat Gentile food. When Peter bridged that gap, a faction of the young church called him on the carpet, and Peter was forced to defend his actions.

*　　*　　*

Brothers, sisters, my family in Christ,
　　some of you have asked why I entered
　　　　the house of Gentiles,
　　　　　　ate their food,
　　and then baptized them into the household of God.
One of you even accused me of profaning
　　the pearl of great price,
　　　　the Gospel of our Lord,
　　　　　　by throwing it before Gentile swine.

81

Friends, hear my story.
    What I did was not done lightly;
        it was done with much prayer
        and with the approval of Christian brothers.
    I was in Joppa, and one day
        I had gone to the rooftop to pray quietly.
    About noon I was hungry,
        but while the food was being prepared,
        I fell into a trance.
    I had a vision:
            heaven opened, and a strange vessel descended.
        It looked like a great sheet,
            held by the four corners;
        inside were all sorts of four-footed beasts
            and reptiles and wild birds.
        Then I heard a voice saying,
            "Get up, Peter, kill and eat."
    I was shocked,
        for the voice seemed to come from heaven,
            but all those beasts were unclean by God's law.
    I answered at once,
        "No, Lord, no, for I've never eaten anything
        unlawful or unclean."
    The voice spoke again,
        "What God has made clean,
        you must not call unclean."
    All this happened three times,
        and then the vision suddenly disappeared
        into heaven.

I didn't know what to make of this;
        it just didn't make sense.
    If this was from God,
        why would God tell me to break the holy law
        he gave to Moses?
    While I puzzled about it,
        I heard shouting outside the gate.

Three men were standing there, asking for me.
Then the Spirit spoke to me,
"Get up, go down, and go with them
without hesitation, for I have sent them."
I went down and found they were Gentiles,
and the story they told me
was even more strange.

They were a soldier and two slaves,
all sent by a Roman centurion named Cornelius.
They told me that Cornelius was a good man
who believed in our God
and was respected by the Jews.
The day before, when Cornelius was praying,
he saw a vision.
An angel of God told him to send for me
to come to his house so he could listen
to what I had to say.
What could I do?
They said Cornelius had had a vision;
I had had a vision.
Cornelius was told to send for me;
I was told to go.
What should I tell the three men?
I turned to my host,
for I was staying in the house of Simon the Tanner.
He nodded, so I called the three men in to eat
and to spend the night.

Simon told me, "All the Jews here on the seacoast
have heard of this Cornelius.
He's a centurion in the Italian Cohort,
a chosen band.
You know these centurions:
the backbone of the Roman army.
They're picked as leaders,
men of good judgment,

not apt to fly off the handle,
able when hard-pressed to stand fast
and die at their post.
But this Cornelius is more than that.
He believes in the one true God,
the living God of Israel.
It's said that he gives alms generously.
He hasn't become a full proselyte:
circumcised, eating Jewish food.
I don't know what would happen to him
in the army if he did.
He holds back from that,
but he is trusted and liked by all the Jews
in Caesarea.
If he says he's had a vision from God,
I'd go and find out."

Simon called in other believers from Joppa,
and we prayed.
Then the Spirit guided Simon and five of the brothers.
"We will go with you.
We will bear witness, along with you,
to the grace of God in Christ our Lord.
If there is danger on the road,
we will share the danger.
God must have a great work
for you to do in Caesarea,
and we will rejoice and praise God for you."
It was settled;
the next morning we would go to Cornelius.

On the road I talked with Cornelius' slaves,
and they told me about the man.
Long ago he threw off the Roman myths
of gods and goddesses who act like spoiled children,
and he rose above the pagan do-as-you-please
morality.

When the army brought him to Judea,
    he learned of our one God,
    the living God,
    and he was drawn by the high moral standards
      of our law.
He became a worshipper of God.
    He prayed; he prayed daily;
    and he had faith that God heard his prayers.
He grew to love our people —
    unlike so many Romans who despise us —
      and he gave alms liberally.
His slaves,
    who certainly get a close look at him,
      call him an upright man.

I wondered what Cornelius would say
    when I entered his house.
What if he offered me food?
    Could I insult him by refusing,
    or must I accept and break our law?
I thought again of my vision.
    Was the Lord telling me to accept all foods?
    Then I remembered that Jesus had once told us
      that what defiles a person
        is not what goes into his mouth.
    It is from within,
      from the human heart,
      that evil intentions come;
    those are what defile a person.
That must be the meaning of the vision:
    the Lord has sent me to Cornelius;
    to obey God I must go.
"Get up, Peter, kill and eat," the voice had said.
It must mean that if Cornelius
    offers me Roman food, God has made it clean.
But can it mean more than food?
What of the Roman himself?

Can it mean that God will make the Gentiles clean,
  that God will accept Gentiles?

We reached Caesarea in the afternoon.
As I entered the house,
  Cornelius himself came up to me,
    a tall man, strong,
      with an air of command.
  Then he fell down at my feet.
I was shocked.
  Roman centurions do not fall down before anyone
    except God or Caesar.
  It would be blasphemy to let him worship me.
  "Stand up," I said, "I am only a mortal."
Then I looked around the room.
  This was no private talk;
    he had called together his relatives
      and his friends to hear what I had to say.

I explained my vision, saying,
  "You already know that it is against the Jewish
    law for me to visit in a Gentile house,
    but God has shown me that I should not
      call anyone unclean.
  So when you sent for me, I came.
Now, may I ask why you sent for me?"

He replied with his vision.
  While he was praying,
    he suddenly saw a man in dazzling clothes.
  The angel said,
    "Cornelius, your prayer has been heard and
      your alms have been remembered before God.
    Send therefore to Joppa and ask for Simon,
      who is called Peter."
Cornelius added, "So now all of us are here
  in the presence of God to listen to all
    that the Lord has commanded you to say."

Did anyone ever have a clearer invitation
       to tell the good news of Jesus Christ?
   I knew this must be from God.
   The Spirit had brought these people to the gospel;
   I must bring the gospel to the people.
I told them of Jesus:
   his baptism,
   his teaching,
   his great signs and works,
   his death, his glorious resurrection,
   his coming day when he will judge
       the living and the dead,
   the promise that everyone who believes in him
       receives forgiveness of sins through his name.

I did not expect —
   I was overwhelmed —
       at what happened.
   While I was still speaking,
       the Holy Spirit fell on all those who heard,
       and they began to speak with tongues,
       praising God,
           just as we had done on the day of Pentecost.

Then I was struck with the full meaning of my vision.
   The vision wasn't about food at all;
       the vision was about people!
   Jesus didn't die on the cross for food;
       he died for people!
   God had accepted these Gentiles,
       just as he had accepted us.
   God makes people clean,
       Gentile and Jew alike,
       clean by the salvation that is in Jesus Christ.
I remembered the words of our Lord,
   "John baptized with water,
       but you will be baptized with the Holy Spirit."

If God gave them the same gift that he gave us,
who was I that I should hinder God?

I turned to the six Jewish believers
who came with me from Joppa.
"Can anyone withhold the water for baptizing
these people who have received the Holy Spirit
just as we have?"
All the men from Joppa answered with one voice,
"God has received them;
God has baptized them with the Holy Spirit;
who are we to refuse?"
I gave the word;
the brothers from Joppa baptized
the new brothers and sisters in Caesarea.
We embraced each other,
Jew and Gentile alike,
in a holy embrace.
We praised God together with joy and thanksgiving.

There was so much that Cornelius and his house
wanted to learn about Jesus,
so much they asked about the believers
here at Jerusalem and in other towns.
They begged us to stay and teach them,
so we stayed for several days.
While we were with them,
they began to spread the news
among their kinfolk and friends,
and soon more new believers were added
to the body.
Then they sent us off to Joppa,
rejoicing that God had given to Gentiles
the repentance that leads to life.

What will happen to Cornelius?
He is a man in the chain of command,

obeying the officers over him
and making decisions about the soldiers
under him.
Now he has a new commander;
he will obey God.
He will make his decisions in the light of his faith
in Jesus our Lord.

Cornelius made a decision to believe in Christ
and to obey him.
I made a decision:
Cornelius had been accepted by God,
and so I must accept Cornelius.
You and I, all of us in God's church,
have made the decision to belong to God
through Jesus Christ.
Yet also you and I have decisions to make each day,
several times each day.
At each fork of the road, we make the decision
to follow the way of Christ or some other way.
At each transaction in the marketplace,
each meeting with a friend,
we make a decision
based on our commitment to Christ
or a decision that backs away
from that commitment.

God grant that each of our decisions
shall show the love of God
embodied in Christ our Lord. Amen.

Luke 2:8-20

The Other Shepherd Speaks

The shepherds came to the manger, actors who play one brief scene and then vanish. Luke tells us they returned, "glorifying and praising God for all they had seen and heard, as it had been told them." Beyond that, we know nothing of their later lives. Yet does any person meet the living Christ and remain unchanged?

*   *   *

Aye, they said we missed it.
   "We missed it," they said,
      and they were right.

We were out in the fields,
   five of us, with the sheep,
      and it was a chilly night.
   I had the early watch;
      the sheep were all settled down.

About midnight I woke Jeremy —
    it was his watch.
I wrapped up in my robe
    and was just about asleep
        when a bright light shone in my face.
"What's that?" I muttered.
    "Can't a man get any rest?"
I rolled over and shut my eyes.
There was a murmur of voices.
    Jeremy shook me.
        "We're going! We're going!
        It's an angel of God. A whole choir of angels!
            saying the Messiah is born,
            the Messiah is born in Bethlehem.
        We're going to see him!"
"You're crazy," I growled.
    "It's some wild dream
        and you're going off on a fool's errand.
    Not me. I've been up all night,
        and now you wake me with a dream like this."
Off they went, the three of them.
    Zeke and I stayed with the sheep,
        and a busy night it was,
            just the two of us, in lambing time.

Before dawn they came back, all excited,
    their faces almost shining.
    "It was an angel, for sure," they said,
        "a whole chorus of angels!"
            And Zeke and I missed it all.

In Bethlehem they found things just as the angel said:
    a family from Nazareth,
        staying in a stable.
    The husband, a carpenter,
        overwhelmed by the angels and everything,
    the mother, young, they said, and nice,

saying she wondered what it all meant —
    visits of angels to her and her husband both,
    telling them words from the prophets.
There was the baby, a fine boy,
    asleep in the manger,
    a baby all the world could love.
But something more:
    a strange peace, they said,
      a strange radiance.
His mother said,
    "I know he's my own dear baby,
      but when I hold him,
        I feel as if I'm holding the whole world
          in my arms —
        the sky and the sea and the green earth
          and all the angels of Heaven."
If only she knew what I know now —
    for how could she hold him?
    It's the other way around.
    He was holding her —
      and holding you and me —
        and all the world —
          in his saving hands!

But that's ahead of my tale.
    The three came back
      and told us what they'd found:
    an everyday scene of a mother and a baby —
      but different —
    with a holy feeling of God at work.
I've learned long since
    that what looks ordinary to me
    doesn't mean ordinary when God goes to work.
I missed it that night, but I learned it later.
The angel told them,
    "This is what was said by the prophet Isaiah,
      'Behold, a virgin shall conceive and bear a son,

and his name shall be called "Emmanuel"
which means, "God with us!" ' "
How could a baby, a tiny baby,
be the mystery of "God with us"?
How could such a great event
happen in such a small place?
And the angels tell it to shepherds, of all people?
When we told the story, the city folk
looked down at us as poor beasts of the field,
with no more sense
then the sheep we take care of.
No one listened,
and we stopped talking about that night.

That was forty years ago.
I was a young man then, just married.
And what I have seen these forty years:
many a sheep and many a long night.
I have seen a man named Jesus.
I saw him break bread and hand it out.
I ate, and we all ate, 5,000 of us.
I saw him heal a lame man,
when I was in Jerusalem for the Passover.
The next Passover,
I saw that same Jesus,
hanging on a cross.
Then I heard stories:
that he was risen — alive —
and I heard another story:
he was that baby I failed to see,
that chilly night forty years ago.

In my heart, I felt him.
Years before, I'd closed my ears to the angels
and shut my eyes to their light,
but now in my heart I felt Jesus,
and knew he is the Messiah, the Savior.

94

In my soul, I felt the mystery
of "God with us."
I don't understand it.
I'm not a great one for books or long speeches.
How the almighty God became "God with us":
flesh of our flesh
in the flesh of that little baby —
bone of our bone
in the bones of that man on the cross.
All I know is
in the fullness of God's time
God sent his son:
sent him right into the center of our life.
God has linked himself to us —
and given us a pattern of true life.
Jesus died, but Jesus rose from the dead;
and he shattered the fear of death,
tore down the barriers
between himself and us.
God wasn't embarrassed to show himself
as a weak little baby.
Aye, if he came in all his power,
we'd have flattened ourselves to the ground.
But how like God to come as a baby:
a baby won't force you to do anything —
no army, no sword,
no strong fist to take you by the arm
and drag you along;
a baby just loves —
and lets you love him,
care for him,
nurture him,
gives the good side of you a chance
to use that goodness.
Is that why God came as a baby?
I don't know.
I only know he came to me —

came to me as the baby,
and the man,
and the almighty God.
He brought into me — inside me —
a revolution,
a change of life,
so that in my weakness
I feel his strength,
and in my fears and failures
I know he loves me,
and in my joys and blessings
I know he cares.

Aye, true, I'm just a shepherd,
and poor,
and people put me down, saying,
"What could a poor man know?"
But the prophets have been poor,
and the people who thought themselves so great
laughed at the prophets —
and they missed the truth.
Aye, they missed the word of God,
because they would not see it in small places
or hear it in plain, simple words.
It's easy to miss the call of God.
We don't look for it in small places,
or in ordinary folk.
Who would have thought a shepherd-boy
could fight the giant Goliath
and become our greatest king — King David?
Who would have thought that angels
would speak to poor shepherds,
or that a baby born in a stable
would be the Savior?

Aye, we missed him then,
because God came to us in ways we did not expect:

not in the capitals of great empires
        nor in the beauty of great temples,
    but in the quiet call of God to human hearts.
I missed it once —
        and God called to me again.
    God grant you eyes that look for him
            in unlikely places
        and ears to listen for his word.
    God grant you never miss his call.

Acts 15:22, 30-41

Silent Silas

There was a man named Silas. We read of him in Acts and in several of the Epistles. Yet in the whole of the New Testament there is not one word from Silas himself: not a word that he said, not a scrap of a letter in his own name. Was he silent? We know he was not. He was a prophet for Christ; he exhorted, taught, preached, prayed, and sang.

Of all that Silas said, what was it and what was it worth? The First Epistle of Peter was written by the hand of Silas. If we were to ask Peter, what might he say?

* * *

Silas?
> Yes, he wrote down that letter for me.
>> He put it into better Greek than I can write,
>> all polished.
> After all, I was a fisherman in Galilee;
>> I learned my Greek in the fish market.

99

Silas was a city man, educated,
a traveler who spoke Greek wherever he went.
He wrote my letter for me
and carried it to the churches in Asia Minor.

You ask what sort of a man he was.
John Mark was like a son to me;
Silas was more like a brother.
That's what I called him in my letter:
a faithful brother.
I met him back in Jerusalem,
when he first became a Christian.
He was a good man, upright, well-respected;
he loved God and lived by the commandments.
He already knew the old Scriptures,
and when he came to faith in Jesus as Lord,
he wanted to know the whole truth
of the Savior.
He had a good mind,
spoke well;
and soon the growing church
looked to him as a leader.
Then there was a fuss up in Antioch.
Most of the new Christians there
had been Gentiles,
and of course they ate Gentile food
and hadn't been circumcised.
To add to that,
Paul and Barnabas went out from Antioch
on a long missionary journey;
to Cyprus, Cilicia, Galatia, Phrygia.
In each town, they went to the Jews first
and then to the Gentiles;
they came back telling how so many pagan
idol-worshippers had turned to faith
in the one true God
and Jesus Christ his Son.

Everything was fine at Antioch
    until some of the brothers who were extra strict
      about the law came there from Jerusalem.
    They raised a storm, saying those new converts
      had to become Jews first —
        circumcision, Jewish food, Jewish dress —
      or they couldn't be real Christians.
    I was there when it happened;
      it made a real row in the Church.
Paul set them straight.
    He saw right to the heart of it,
      that salvation is the gift of God's grace in Christ,
      received by faith alone.
      Basing salvation on anything else
        would undercut the Gospel.

The Church at Antioch sent Paul and Barnabas
    down to Jerusalem, and we had a big council.
    I told how God had sent me
      to carry the gospel to the Gentile Cornelius.
    The apostles and elders agreed that Paul was right;
      we are saved by grace,
        not by keeping rules,
      and we will not require new believers
        to take on the whole law of Moses.
We wrote a letter to Antioch
    and the other new churches.
    But who would carry the letter?
    We had to send men of such character
      and such standing in the church
        that it would be clear they spoke
        with the authority of the apostles,
          the elders, and the whole church.
    We chose carefully,
      and Silas was one of our men.
Silas was well received,
      for he was far more than a letter-carrier.

He spoke as a prophet,
    taught the believers,
        encouraged and strengthened them.
He stayed there some time,
        bringing peace to that church;
    they gave him a loving send-off
        when he came home to Jerusalem.

Silas' next big step came when Paul sent for him.
    Paul and Barnabas had planned another mission,
        but they split over taking Mark with them again.
Paul needed a new partner.
    During that time in Antioch,
        Paul had learned Silas' worth,
           and they knew they could work together.
    Besides, Silas came from the Jerusalem church,
        and he had their blessing.
    More, he was a Roman citizen,
        so he could go anywhere in the whole Empire.
They started off,
    and it turned into a long trip.
    They walked the length of Syria,
        then Asia Minor from one end to the other,
        strengthening the churches.
    Then Paul had a vision calling them to Macedonia;
        so they did not hesitate,
           and they crossed over to Europe.

At Philippi,
    their first city in Europe,
        they made a good start
           and gathered a new church.
    Then a few greedy men raised a mob
        and had them seized, beaten, and jailed.
    At midnight, in jail,
        their feet cramped in the stocks,
           their backs bloody from the beating,
             what would they do?

The other prisoners expected moaning and cursing,
    but Paul and Silas were singing hymns
        and praying to God.
The other prisoners, awed, were listening.
Silas was not a man to whimper,
    or quit,
        or lost faith.

Would Paul have been as strong
    without Silas to pray with him,
        sing with him,
            support and encourage him?
When you build a fire,
    and you get down to one log,
        it will go out.
But if you have two logs side by side,
    they shine the heat back and forth
        and the fire keeps burning between them.
I think that's one reason our Lord brought us
    together in his church:
        to warm each other's faith.
I'm sure that night in jail,
    Silas and Paul fed each other's fires
        of hope and faith.

Well, before the night was over,
    the jailer was converted,
        and the next day Paul and Silas left town.
At Thessalonica they gathered a church,
    but then they were driven out.
The same happened at Berea,
    but there Paul left Silas and Timothy behind
        to teach the new Christians.
Paul really trusted both of them.
Later, when they wrote to the church at Thessalonica,
    they wrote as a team:
        Paul, Silas, and Timothy.

They had a record to be proud of:
"Our message of the gospel came to you
         not in word only,
      but also in power and in the Holy Spirit
         and with full conviction;
      just as you know what kind of persons
         we proved to be among you for your sake."
That's the way all three of them were:
         servants of Christ
      who had proved themselves to be
         all that they should be.

Silas joined Paul again in Corinth,
      and they worked there for more than a year.
   Later, when Paul wrote to Corinth,
      he put Silas on an equal footing with himself,
   reminding the Corinthians of
         "the Son of God, Jesus Christ,
            whom we proclaimed among you,
            Silas and Timothy and I."
They build monuments to generals,
      chisel their names in stone,
   but no general ever won a battle
      without the captains and sergeants
         and soldiers in the thick of the fight.
   I don't think Paul could have done as much
      without Silas and Timothy and the others.
   There's no doubt Silas was a valued member
      of Paul's team.

Aye, and Silas is a valued helper to me.
   For, ten years later,
         our paths have crossed again,
            in Rome.
We've worked together.
   He's written down my letter in good Greek,
   and I've just sent him off

to carry it to the churches of Asia Minor —
some of them the same churches he and Paul
visited on that great trip together.

I wrote he is a faithful brother;
he's all that and more.
You asked, "What did he say?
Why don't we know his words?"
We don't need to know all his exact words
to know what he stood for.
As a leader in the church at Jerusalem,
he stood for Christ.
As a companion of Paul,
he stood for the same good news
of the saving grace of God in Christ.
As my helper,
he wrote of faith in Christ,
of strength and comfort in persecution.
His words and his work
were like beams of the church,
that give strength to the whole structure.
You know my name, Old Peter,
and you know some of my words.
You know Silas' name.
But it's not our names that matter,
but what we did and what we stood for,
as brothers under Jesus Christ.
There's many a Christian whose words
aren't written
and whose name we don't know,
but who has spoken a word
that comforted the sorrowing,
cheered the sad,
gave hope in time of despair,
led a child into God's family,
encouraged the faltering,
or opened the truth to someone seeking it.

Each of those lives will touch another,
    and those in turn will touch still others;
    so the words of that unknown Christian
      who started the chain
        will never be lost.

Paul, Silas, Timothy —
    Yes, and me, Peter —
    and you —
    Yes. You.
    Will you speak a word
        that lifts someone up in the love of Christ?
    That word shall never be lost.

A Slave, A Jailer,
A Child Of God

We have only a bare-bones mention of the Philippian jailer. He received Paul and Silas, beaten and bleeding; he fastened them in the painful stocks; after his conversion, he personally dressed their wounds and then fed them at his own table. What other changes grew from the jailer's new Christian faith? Let us attempt to stretch some living flesh over those bare bones.

* * *

Call me Quintus,
       but my name doesn't matter.
    Most people just see me as a slave,
       a piece of the house furniture,
          nothing more.
My master is the town jailer,
        just that,
       and most people don't bother to call his name:
       he's the jailer, nothing more.

But there is more.
    That's all he was
    and all I was,
        but now there is more.
He's a child of God:
    still the jailer,
    but now a child of God.
And I'm a child of God:
    still a slave,
    but now a child of God.

You raise an eyebrow?
    I'll tell you how it came about,
    and I'll tell you what it means.

This city of ours, Philippi, was an old city,
    founded by Philip of Macedon,
        father of Alexander the Great.
The Romans conquered it 200 years ago
    and pretty well wrecked what was there.
Then some 80 years ago came Octavian
    (you know him as the Emperor Augustus),
    and here he defeated Brutus and Cassius,
        the men who murdered his uncle, Julius Caesar.
Afterwards, he settled his veterans here
    and made the city a Roman colony,
        giving its freemen the status of Roman citizens.
It gave Rome a good military base,
    and it gave the city a new start.

That's how my master came here.
    He was a veteran of the Roman legions,
        and he rose to the rank of centurion;
            then he retired here.
    All the town officials are veterans;
        one of them, his old commander,
            gave him the office of jailer.

It's a good living;
   he's not rich,
      but he has a good house,
      enough money to support his family
      and to keep a half-dozen servants.

He was a fair enough master, but strict;
   all the old army men were trained to be strict.
Most were honest and fair.
They let you know their rules:
   obey orders, and you'd be all right;
   break orders, and be ready for punishment.
The training of those Roman legionnaires
   didn't include very much
      of the milk of human kindness.

But back to my story.
   A man called Paul, a Jew,
      and Silas, another Jew,
      and two others, Timothy and Luke,
         Greeks or part-Greeks,
      came here.

Here's the way Luke told me the start of it.
   "We set sail from Troas
      and took a straight course to Samothrace,
      the following day to Neapolis,
      and from there to Philippi.
   We remained in this city for some days.
   On the Sabbath day we went outside the gate
      by the river,
      where we supposed there was a place of prayer."
   — that is, a Jewish place of prayer:
      there weren't enough Jews in Philippi
         to have a synagogue.
"A certain woman named Lydia,
   a worshipper of God, was listening to us."

She's a Greek from Thyatira,
    where they know the business
    of making purple cloth.
She's the merchant for it here,
    a real smart business woman,
    well-respected,
    a widow with a big household.
She was looking for something,
    a true God, not some patchy idol.
That's why she was praying
    with the Jewish women,
        seeking a most high God.
"The Lord opened her heart to listen eagerly
to what was said by Paul.
When she and her household were baptized,
*   she urged us, saying, 'If you have judged me*
*   to be faithful to the Lord,*
*   come and stay at my home.' "*
That's how it went for a while:
    Paul and Silas preaching in the city every day,
    going out to the place by the river to pray,
    and teaching the believers more about Jesus.

But then they ran into trouble.
    Luke said,
    "We met a slave girl who had a spirit of divination
    and brought her owners a great deal of money
    by fortune-telling.
    While she followed Paul and us, she would cry out,
    'These men are slaves of the Most High God,
    who proclaim to you a way of salvation.'
    But Paul was very much annoyed."
Not annoyed that she shouted
    they were servants of the Most High God
    and that they told people the way of salvation;
that's what Paul himself said
        every time he preached.

Paul was annoyed at the way her owners
were exploiting her.
There she was, tormented in spirit,
and her owners were making money
from her misery.
"Paul turned and said to the spirit,
'I order you in the name of Jesus Christ
to come out of her.'
And it came out that very hour."
The girl was set free
from that slavery of the spirit,
but she was still a slave,
a piece of property —
and it didn't suit her owners one bit.
As they saw it,
Paul had interfered with their property.

Luke told me the girl's owners seized Paul and Silas,
dragged them before the magistrates
in the marketplace, and said,
"These men are disturbing our city;
they are Jews
and are advocating customs
that are not lawful for us as Romans
to adopt or observe."
It was a pack of lies, of course,
but the mob was on their side:
they saw Paul and Silas as vagabond Jews,
spreading some kind of perverse superstition —
and there's a lot of anti-Jewish feeling
among Romans — always has been.

The magistrates are proud men:
proud of being Romans
and scornful of everyone else.
They took the accusations at face value
and didn't bother looking for the truth.

If they'd asked,
    they would have found that Paul and Silas
        were Roman citizens
        and that the charges were false.
    The magistrates said Roman citizens
        shouldn't be bothered by strolling peddlers
            of an outlandish religion:
            such people must be taught
                to keep their proper place.
    So they tore the robes from Paul and Silas
        and ordered them beaten with rods.
The lictors beat them pretty badly;
        then they turned them over to my master
        with orders to keep them safely.

Well, my master was a strict man.
    He had his orders,
        and he carried them out strictly.
    He told the guards to throw them
        into the innermost part of the prison
        and fasten their legs in the stocks.
    He didn't care that the blood was flowing
        from the stripes on their bare backs
            or that the stocks hurt their legs.
    He didn't bother giving them food.
    They were just a pair of tramps,
        and he wasn't there to coddle them;
        that was none of his business.

What would you expect Paul and Silas to do?
    The other prisoners expected
        to hear groaning and cursing,
            what with the pain of their backs
                and the cramping of their legs,
        but what came out from the middle of the jail
            was prayer to God
                and the singing of hymns.

The others wondered about those two men:
    wondered with a kind of awe.

Just then, at midnight, an earthquake hit;
    rocked the stones, it did,
        so the chains pulled loose from the wall
            and the door flew open;
        then the stones settled back.
    This is earthquake country,
        and it's funny what a quake will do
            to old stone walls.

My master woke up,
    ran to the jail,
        found the door open,
            and thought, of course,
                the prisoners were all gone.
    You know these Roman soldiers,
        brought up on discipline
            and their sense of honor.
    When they've failed in their duty,
        their own course of honor is suicide.

The master couldn't see into the jail,
    but Paul, inside,
        saw him outlined in the doorway,
            drawing his sword to kill himself.
    Paul shouted, "Do not harm yourself,
        for we are all here."
There was something uncanny about those two men;
    they had kept the other prisoners there, too.
    With the jailer dead,
        they'd all have a better chance of escaping,
        but Paul cared about him,
            kept him alive,
                after the way Paul had been treated.

My master called for me to bring a light,
    and he rushed in.
  Trembling with fear,
    he fell down before Paul and Silas.
  Roman jailers don't bow down before prisoners,
    but he did.
  These men had saved his life.
  He'd treated them like dogs,
    yet they cared enough to keep him from suicide,
    and then they told him of the love of God.
What kind of men were these?
  My master had heard the reports around town,
    that they spoke of salvation,
    of a new life through the living God.
  Now he knew that they had something real,
    and he needed it.
  He brought them outside and asked,
    "Sirs, what must I do to be saved?"
  They answered,
    "Believe on the Lord Jesus,
      and you will be saved,
        you and your household."
  They my master called us all together —
    his wife, children, slaves, guards —
  and Paul told us the whole story,
    the whole good news of Jesus Christ:
    the Son of God,
    his miracles and signs,
    his teachings,
    his crucifixion for our sins,
    his rising from the dead,
    his living power with his people.
  Paul told us of a new life in Christ,
    of being born anew as children of God.

That night my master became a child of God.
  Lydia had been searching for God,
    and she welcomed the Gospel.

My master was a different kind of man.
    He'd lived a hard life and he had a tough hide.
    It took an earthquake
        and a close escape from suicide
        to make him think of God and of salvation —
        and God used the same Gospel
            to turn him into a new person.

I saw the change, and everyone there saw it.
    We saw Paul and Silas,
        examples of the grace and love of God.
    We saw my master:
        the change was starting already.
    He brought Paul and Silas into his house,
        took a basin of water,
        washed their wounds and soothed them with oil.
    He could have told any servant to do it;
        he did it himself,
            and he did it with tenderness —
        something I'd never seen in him before.
    He'd always had a callous shell.
        If the magistrates told him to kill, he killed.
        If he received men who were bleeding,
            he didn't care; that was their tough luck.
    Now he was a new master,
        a man of compassion.
    One could say, "He washed and was washed.
        He washed their stripes,
            and he himself was washed from his sins."
    The Spirit of God entered him.
        He believed in Jesus:
        by the love of Jesus he became a new man,
            and he showed it.
    The change in him was spontaneous,
            and he lived it in a down-to-earth way.
        He called for the cook — he was still master —
        and fed Paul and Silas at his own table.

And I?
    I felt the change, too.
    A burden was lifted within me.
    I'm a slave, but I'm free inside,
        free by the grace of God.

There's a difference in the way my master treats us.
    He has a job, and he wants it done;
        but he's no longer harsh.
    He cares.
    He has a new care
        in the way he treats the prisoners,
        and he sends food to the hungry in town.
    And we share a love;
        we share a joy.

Yes, he's still the jailer,
        and I'm still Quintus the slave,
            but we are more.
We are children of God.

Luke 7:1-10
1 Kings 8:23, 41-43

Unlimited God, Unlimited Love

The small house in Jerusalem was overcrowded with guests, for this was the house where Paul and his companions stayed on his last trip to the holy city. Seated on the floor were two men from Ephesus in Asia Minor, Tychicus and Trophimus; near them were Aristarchus and Secundus from northern Greece, then Sopater from Berea and Gaius from Derbe; beside the door sat their host, Mnason, an early disciple of Christ from the Island of Cyprus. Over to the side another man bent over a small table, writing on a roll of papyrus.

*　　*　　*

The door opened and a young man entered.
　　Timothy spoke to the men in the circle
　　　　and then walked over to the writing desk.
　　　　"Greetings, Luke,
　　　　　　it's good to see you back from Galilee.

We've prayed for your safety.
Our Lord Jesus has many there who love Him —
    but there are also those
        who are not very gentle with His followers,
        especially a Greek.
What have you learned on your trip?''

Luke laid down his pen and stretched his arms.
''I'm glad I went.
    It's hard to sit here in Jerusalem, just waiting,
        with Paul in prison in Caesarea,
            not knowing when he will be put on trial.
    So I've been trying to talk with people
        who knew Jesus
        and write down what they said.
This trip to Galilee was marvelous, marvelous.
    The disciples there led me to men and women
        our Lord had healed — of dozens of diseases —
            palsy, leprosy, blindness, paralysis —
                some near death.
As a physician, I know those cases are hopeless,
    yet there the people were,
        alive, in good health;
            and their families attest to their cure.
I met so many people Jesus had lifted up in spirit:
    his forgiveness changed their lives.
It's been nearly thirty years,
    and there are still so many
        to whom he has given hope,
            so many who remember his compassion.

''Here, listen to what I've just written.''
After Jesus had finished all his sayings in the hearing of
the people, he entered Capernaum. A centurion was there
who had a slave whom he valued highly, and who was ill
and close to death. When he heard about Jesus, he sent
some Jewish elders to him, asking him to come and heal

118

his slave. When they came to Jesus, they appealed to him earnestly, saying, "He is worthy of having you do this for him, for he loves our people, and it is he who built our synagogue for us." And Jesus went with them, but when he was not far from the house, the centurion sent friends to say to him, "Lord, do not trouble yourself, for I am not worthy to have you come under my roof; therefore I did not presume to come to you. But only speak the word, and let my servant be healed. For I also am a man set under authority, with soldiers under me; and I say to one, 'Go,' and he goes, and to another, 'Come,' and he comes, and to my slave, 'Do this,' and he does it." When Jesus heard this, he was amazed at him, and turning to the crowd that followed him, he said, "I tell you, not even in Israel have I found such faith." When those who had been sent returned to the house, they found the slave in good health.

Sopater spoke up.
  "Tell us more, Luke.
  Did you meet any of those people?"
"Yes, I met the centurion,
  and I met one of the elders he sent to Jesus.
    It was the elder who told me the details.
That centurion is a remarkable man.
  No one gets to be a Roman centurion
    unless he is very capable,
      but this man is unusual.
  He's about 70 now, still in command,
    and a leader of the Christians in Capernaum.
  He's unusual in his compassion,
    not hard and callous like so many Roman soldiers.
  Some Romans treat their slaves like animals
      or things,
        tools to be used and then thrown away.
  This man cared about his slave,
    loved the slave and his family.

When the slave was paralyzed and in pain,
        the centurion cared,
                and he went asking for help.
He was unusual, too, in his friendship with Jesus.
    Most Roman soldiers despise Jews as weak,
        a subject people.
    They know the Jews hate them,
        and they hate right back.
    This man saw the goodness of the Jews,
        and he realized that their goodness
                came from their faith in the one true God.
    He became a worshipper of God,
        a friend to the Jews in Capernaum.
    He dug into his own pocket to build their synagogue,
        and they in turn accepted him as a friend.
And he is humble.
    You don't expect a Roman officer to be humble —
        they are trained to command —
        but he knew how to recognize true greatness.
    He had heard how Jesus had healed other people,
        right there in Capernaum,
                and he didn't try to command Jesus.
    He sent Jewish elders,
            thinking they might have more influence than he;
        and they in turn went
                because they liked him and respected him.
He was considerate, too.
    He knew Jesus would be criticized
            if he entered a Gentile house,
        so — to spare Jesus —
    he said he was unworthy for Jesus to come,
        and he asked Jesus to heal from where he was.
Above all, the man had faith.
    He was a man of authority,
        and he knew his authority produced results.
    He reasoned that Jesus had greater authority,
        authority over healing,
        power over life and death.

He said with perfect confidence,
    'Lord, I know you can do this at a distance.'
He didn't need to see medical treatment;
    he didn't even need to see Jesus in person:
    Jesus could do it.
Many, many people were demanding
    that Jesus show them visible signs
        before they would believe:
    this man had real faith, and Jesus answered it —
        praised it, in fact.
He healed the man's servant,
    and he said he had not found such faith
    in native Israelites."

Mnason, their host, raised a question.
"Luke, I've heard that story.
    I haven't met the centurion,
        but I've heard it from John and from Peter
        and from Matthew, who were there.
    But what does it mean for us?
        What lesson do you think the Lord has for us?"

Luke thought for a moment.
    "The first lesson I see is the greatness of God,
        the unlimited power of Christ.
    We physicians need to see a patient,
        examine him carefully,
            touch him,
                treat him with potions and ointments.
    Even then,
        there are so many things we cannot cure.
            We learn our limits.
    Jesus was not limited to medicines,
        or to the touch of his hand.
    He was not limited by space:
        he was a mile away.
        Across that mile he spoke a word,
            and the man was healed.

"The greatness of the centurion
　　was that he realized the power of Jesus
　　was not limited by distance.
　We're finding now that his power
　　is not limited by time.
　It's thirty years since Jesus died and rose.
　　His power is as great now,
　　and his life fills our souls with a new birth.

"His power is unlimited,
　　and his grace, his love, is unlimited.
　The centurion is a Roman, not a Jew;
　　he worshipped God,
　　　　but he had not taken the step of becoming
　　　　a full convert.
　Jesus didn't hold back.
　　He listened to the man's need.
　It was one of the first times Jesus broke out
　　of the tight-closed walls of Judaism.
　God's love, God's good news,
　　is not limited to any one people.
　Look at us here in Mnason's house:
　　some of us Jews,
　　　　some of us Greeks,
　　　　　　Timothy half-and-half.
　That Roman centurion is now a believer.
　God's love doesn't depend on ancestry,
　　or language,
　　　　or color,
　　　　　　or education,
　　　　　　　　or wealth.
　There is one gospel, one good news —
　　and only one —
　　　　for all the nations of the earth:
　　　　the gracious love of God who gives salvation
　　　　　　to all who come to him in faith.
　That gracious love has no limits."

Timothy nodded his head.
"Yes, that gracious love of God has no limits.
We came here as companions of Paul,
    and this is the one gospel we have proclaimed
    along with him:
God's free gift of life, of faith,
    forgiveness, love, salvation —
    unlimited gift —
        to all who come to Him in faith.
Yet there are so many who try to limit God.
Romans trot out their old gods for ceremonies,
    but that has nothing to do
    with the way they run their government.
Greeks write poetry to gods on Olympus,
    but keep them out of their business
    in the marketplace.
The army tries to be god:
    it builds stronger spears, harder shields,
    bigger warships,
    more powerful battering rams,
        as if this will rule the world —
    and forgets it is God's world."

Luke agreed.
"Yes, so many would try to limit God's power,
    keep His power out of their affairs,
        or claim His power as their own.
And so many forget God's unlimited love.
    Each difference becomes prejudice,
    and prejudice leads to oppression,
    and oppression begets hatred.
Rome conquers a country;
    the Roman minority holds the majority as slaves,
        tells them where to live,
        how to work, whom to marry;
        they have no vote, no power.

Can we who know the love of God
  ever agree to such a system?
Suppose the army builds that battering ram —
  even one that can wipe out whole cities.
Would it ever be right to use it?
How can they say another nation is unfit to live,
  when God's compassion is unlimited,
    offered to all peoples?

"We are strangers here in Jerusalem,
  where King Solomon built his temple
    and offered this prayer at its dedication:
    O Lord, God of Israel, there is no God like you in
    heaven above or on earth beneath, keeping covenant
    and steadfast love for your servants who walk before
    you with all their heart ... when a foreigner, who is
    not of your people Israel, comes from a distant land
    because of your name — for they shall hear of your
    great name, your mighty hand, and your outstretched
    arm — when a foreigner comes and prays toward this
    house, then hear in heaven your dwelling place, and do
    according to all that the foreigner calls to you, so that
    all the peoples of the earth may know your name and
    fear you, as do your people Israel ...
This is a world of strangers,
  some carried off as slaves and captives,
    others travelling for commerce
      or just to earn their bread,
  still others — many others —
    fleeing from their homelands as refugees.
Christ our Lord fed the hungry,
  healed the sick,
    forgave the repentant:
can we refuse food for the starving,
  comfort and acceptance for the lonely,
    sanctuary for the oppressed?

Christ our Lord forgave those
　　who nailed Him to the cross;
　can we refuse to love our enemy?

"The Lord our God is unlimited;
　　how can we limit our praise?
The love of God is unlimited;
　　how can we limit whom we will help,
　　　or whom we will love?"

Acts 6:1-6; 8:4-6, 26-40

Philip: The Non-Organization Man

Close your eyes for a moment. Let your mind take you back 1,940 years. You are in Caesarea, a seacoast city in Palestine, and you are in the house of a man named Philip.

The house is so crowded you can hardly get in, for every Christian in town has come to meet Philip's houseguest, Paul, already revered as the great missionary and apostle. Are you ready for what happens when Philip's four daughters, all prophets, announce that the famous apostle is wrong and that he must change his plans?

*　　*　　*

You're shocked at Philip's daughters?
　　I'm not.
You're shocked at Philip's daughters
　　because they dared to tell Paul, of all people,
　　　　to turn around and change his plans?

127

You're shocked at Philip for letting his daughters
   talk that way —
      tell one of the leading men of the church that he
         might be wrong?
You and I both know better than to be surprised.
   After all, they're Philip's daughters.
   I've known them since they were babies.
   They've grown up watching their father always
      do things his way —
      maybe not the way the rest of the church
        goes about its work,
           but it's Philip's way.
If those girls kept their mouths shut
      when the Holy Spirit gave them something to say,
      they wouldn't be Philip's daughters.
   Philip has always looked for direction from the Spirit,
      and the Spirit has led him into some strange places.

I first met Philip in Jerusalem,
   when we were both new Christians,
      both sharing our newly found joy in Christ.
Even then, Philip was walking a different path.
Start with his name, a Greek name.
   He was raised in a Greek city,
      spoke Greek better than he did Hebrew.
   When he moved to Jerusalem,
      he joined a Greek-speaking synagogue.
You know the prejudice in Jerusalem.
   The native Judeans, speaking Hebrew,
      puff themselves up as the only true Jews,
      and they look down on the Greek-speakers
        as not quite good enough.
The Gospel is the Gospel.
   The power of God brought new life
      to people with a Galilean accent,
      to those who spoke the best Hebrew,
        and to Greek-speakers, too.

Soon the church had a large number of Greek-speaking
    members, but they had problems.
        Most of the Grecians were poor.
        Jerusalem society had pushed them down
            into the lowest jobs.
        The widows among them, especially,
            had nowhere to turn.
We believers were giving food to the poor,
    but the Grecians had been shoved aside so long
        that they were afraid the same thing
            would happen in the church:
                their widows would be left out of the distribution.
That's when the church showed the breadth of its love.
    The apostles had their hands full
        teaching the words of Jesus,
        and they knew they couldn't run everything.
    They asked us to choose seven deacons
            to take care of the food,
        and — this was the big step — all seven we chose
            were Greek-speakers.
    We showed that we loved the Grecians
        and trusted them to take care of everybody.
    The prejudices of Jerusalem society
        had no place in our Church.
Philip was one of the seven,
    and I was one of many who voted for him.
    The apostles had asked for "men of good standing,
        full of the Spirit and of wisdom."
    Philip lived up to that then; he lives up to it now.

I said the Holy Spirit led Philip into some strange places.
The first was Samaria.
    Jews weren't welcome in Samaria,
        and most good Jews wouldn't set foot there.
    Jesus was different:
        he went there and he taught there,
            but some towns made it plain he wasn't wanted.

And if Jesus himself wasn't wanted,
    what chance had his followers?
Philip didn't go just to the edge of Samaria;
    he went straight to the capital city, Samaria itself.
He preached the good news of Jesus the Christ.
He declared the power of Jesus to give life;
    and Samaritans accepted that new life with joy.
He proclaimed the power of Christ to heal body and soul,
    and people were healed in body, mind, and soul.
He baptized Samaritans, men and women,
    and received them as sisters and brothers in Christ.
I was still in Jerusalem when we heard that Philip
    had taken the gospel of salvation to Samaritans:
    Samaritans, of all the unlikely people!
Peter and John went down to see what was going on,
    and through them the Holy Spirit confirmed the
    great work Philip had begun.

Philip's next place was even more strange.
    An angel sent him to the road that leads down to Gaza.
    That didn't make sense.
Most of the first Christians went to Jewish cities
    and preached the Gospel to our fellow Jews,
        but this road to Gaza went through wilderness.
Did the angel expect Deacon Philip to preach the gospel
    to thorn bushes?
No, God had a better plan.
    Along came a chariot carrying an Ethiopian,
        a high official, treasurer of the Queen of Ethiopia.
    He was an almost-convert to Judaism.
    He had been to Jerusalem to worship,
        but he could only be an almost-convert,
        for he was a eunuch,
        and no eunuch was accepted in the household of
        Israel.
Should Philip approach this foreigner?
    This man of a different race?
    This man who could never be accepted as a full Jew?

Didn't Christ come to the Jews,
and were not all the apostles Jews,
and were not all the believers Jews,
or at least half-Jews, like those Samaritans?
Philip told me later he could feel the Holy Spirit say,
"Go over to this chariot and join it."
What! How?
Would this high official, with his servants,
stop his chariot at Philip's request?
Philip went to the chariot and ran alongside it,
keeping pace with the horses.
He heard the man reading from the scroll
of the Prophet Isaiah.
Like a sheep he was led to the slaughter,
and like a lamb silent before his shearer,
so he does not open his mouth.
To Philip, that prophecy spoke of only one person,
Jesus, the Messiah.
"Do you understand what you are reading?" Philip
asked.
"How can I, unless somebody guides me?" confessed the
Ethiopian,
and he invited Philip to join him in his chariot.
There Philip taught the man the good news of Jesus,
and when the man believed, and asked for baptism,
Philip baptized him in the name of Christ.
See what Philip had done.
He was the first to take the gospel to Samaritans,
surprising the Apostles,
who at first had gone only to good Jews.
Now he had gone even farther,
to a foreigner,
to a man who could never be accepted as a Jew.
The Holy Spirit had taken him to places where no
decent Jew would go,
and where the apostles had not thought of going.

He had shown that the gospel has no limits —
no limits of place,
no limits of race,
no limits of rich or poor.
The gospel is for all who will come to Jesus Christ.

Where would Philip go then?
Back to Jerusalem with the rest of the deacons?
No, Philip was led by the Spirit to another improbable
place.
He went to Azotus.
You know that's on the seacoast,
in what once was Philistine territory.
Then he worked his way up the coast,
teaching of Jesus in every town along the way.
That's how he first came here to Caesarea,
where he's living now.
Sure, it's an impressive city, with its big buildings,
Governor's palace, fortress, all you'd expect in the
Roman capital for Palestine.
All those Roman soldiers and officials didn't make it
a popular place for Jews,
especially a Jew like Philip, who was preaching
the crucified Jesus as the new King of Glory!
But take another look at the people of Caesarea:
a mixed population — Romans, Jews, Greeks, Syrians,
descendants of the onetime Phoenicians,
sailors, travellers, merchants from all the world
docking at its port.
The Spirit showed Philip a worldwide mission field,
a chance to teach the Gospel to people who would
scatter it in every direction.
I moved here a couple of years later,
and by then, Philip's converts —
that's many of our church here —
were on ships bound for every port in the world.

That's the way Philip had been for the last 20 years:
doing things his way,
not always the way of the rest of the Church.

Yes, there is a confrontation.
Paul came to Caesarea on his way to Jerusalem.
And he's staying at Philip's house —
it's always open to travelling Christians.
The prophet Agabus came down.
Many years before, in Antioch,
Paul had listened to Agabus' prophecy,
and Paul had done what Agabus said.
Now Agabus had a different word for Paul.
He took Paul's belt,
tied his own hands and feet with the belt, and said,
"Paul, this is how the Jews at Jerusalem will tie
you and hand you over to the Romans."
Paul had made up his mind. He was going to Jerusalem.
Right or wrong, prophet or no prophet,
he was going to Jerusalem.
That's when Philip's daughters spoke up.
They begged Paul not to go to Jerusalem.
You know the rest.
You've heard Paul's answer.
He is determined to go to Jerusalem.

Is it a shame for those four young women to tell the
great apostle he is wrong?
For years I've watched Philip listen to the Holy Spirit,
and go where the Spirit sends him —
even to places unexpected by him,
and more surprising to others.
If his daughters dare to correct Paul,
I know they've learned from their father
to listen to the Spirit,
and to say whatever the Spirit gives them to say.

What about us?
Let's reverse our time-travel and come back to today,
        to the year 1996.
Do we always do things
        just the way the church has always done them,
                or do we ask what new task God has for us?
    Do we have the love and the enthusiasm
        to follow the impulse of God's Spirit?
    Do we have the faith and the courage to do the
        unexpected and the unplanned,
                even perhaps the unpopular,
                        for the glory of God?
    Do we have the Biblical knowledge
        to challenge the Church
                to be faithful to the Word of God?
    Do we have the love to go to someone in trouble
        and speak freely of God's love,
                and then put that love into action?
    Are we ready to seek out God's guidance
        and follow God's direction,
                out of the love of Jesus Christ our Lord?

Acts 26:1-29

Why, Paul, Why?

The place is a dungeon in Caesarea, a seacoast city, Roman administrative center for Palestine. Seven men, their wrists chained, slump against the walls. An eighth man, small, stooped, his eyes alert, stands facing his visitor.

* * *

Why, Paul, why?
   As you stand there
      with chains hanging from your wrists,
   why?
   What has this business done for you?
   What do you have against me,
      that you wish me to become a Christian?
   Should I end up like you,
      beaten, in jail, or driven from city to city?

You've been in jail here at Caesarea for two years.
It began when you went to Jerusalem to worship.

Your enemies,
     some of your own people,
     found you in the Temple.
They raised a riot,
     dragged you outside,
       beat you and threw stones at you.
     They'd have killed you in another minute
       if the Roman soldiers hadn't rescued you.
Then, bruised,
     with blood running down your face,
you stood there,
silenced the mob with a wave of your hand,
     and told them of the risen Christ
       who appeared to you on the road to Damascus.
I was amazed that they listened to you at all,
     but listen they did
       until you said the Messiah
         had sent you to the Gentiles.
That was too much;
     it started another riot.

You have a way, Paul, of starting riots.
     The very next day they brought you
       before the high priests and the council.
     You began again with the resurrection of Jesus,
       saying, "I am on trial concerning the hope
       of the resurrection of the dead."
To you, these are two inseparable realities:
     Jesus is the Messiah,
       the fulfillment of all your hopes,
     and Jesus is raised from the dead
       and is alive.
But to your listeners, this was cause for another riot.
The council divided itself between Pharisees,
     who believe in a resurrection,
       and Sadducees, who deny it,
         two sides fighting each other
          and about to tear you into pieces.

Even Roman power couldn't keep you in Jerusalem.
    Forty men took a vow not to eat
        until they had killed you:
            I guess they got pretty hungry.
    When the Roman tribune heard of the plot,
        he sent 470 soldiers to escort you to Caesarea.

There you were on the seacoast,
        in the court of the Roman governor Felix.
    In your trial before him,
        you rested your case again on the hope
            of Jesus' resurrection.
    Felix knew you were innocent of any crime,
        but that didn't do you much good.
            He kept you in jail for two full years.
Oh, he was somewhat interested in what you believe.
    He sent for you several times
        to hear about your faith,
    but when you talked of justice
        and the forgiveness of sins,
            that rascal's guilty conscience pulled him back.
    Besides, the greedy schemer was hoping for a bribe.
        As for you, you stayed in jail.

That's just the last two years.
    You've been in trouble before, Paul,
        ever since you became a Christian.
    You had to escape from Damascus
        in a basket lowered over the city wall.
    On your missionary journeys you've been stoned,
        beaten with rods, and jailed.
    You've gone through all sorts of hardships
        for that faith of yours.
    Why, Paul?
        Why do you do this to yourself?

This new governor, Festus, is an honest man,
        but he's new.

He doesn't know anything yet about Judaism
  or the prophets or Christianity.
That's why he invited Herod Agrippa
  to hear you today.
We know what you said to him, Paul.
  There is sheer drama
    in your appearance before Agrippa.
His great-grandfather was Herod the Great,
  king when Jesus was born.
His grandfather murdered John the Baptist
  and sent Jesus back to Pilate.
His father imprisoned Peter and killed James.
Now you face him in the elegant Hall of Audience,
  built by his great-grandfather.
He and his sister wear the purple robes of royalty;
Festus has his scarlet robe as Roman governor.
His officials are there,
  with an honor guard of centurions and legionnaires.
There you stand, Paul,
    small, stooped,
    chains dangling about your gnarled hands.
But you are not impressed by Agrippa
  or awed by Roman power.
When you speak,
    your expression is magnetic,
    your eyes glint with majesty,
    and your voice cuts through all the pomp
      and pretentiousness to center on one person:
    Jesus Christ,
      the first to rise from the dead,
        to proclaim light and life
        to everyone who turns to him in faith.

I've sensed a resilience in you Christians
  who believe in the resurrection,
  as if that Lord you believe in
    has released your untapped energies.

I've seen it in others;
    when they were at the limits of their endurance,
        their faith infused them
        with strength beyond their own.
You've shown it so often, Paul,
    and you showed it in your answer to Agrippa,
    "I pray to God that not only you
        but also all who are listening to me today
        might become such as I am —
           except for these chains."

Yes, Paul, that's for you.
    That's your commitment to Jesus Christ.
From the time of your meeting with him
        on the road to Damascus,
    you have known only one master.
But why, Paul, do you want to make me a Christian?
I've seen all the trouble,
        dangers,
           hardships
               it's brought you.
Why do you wish this for me?

Is your answer the same for me as it is for yourself,
    that you want me to know the same hope,
        the same glory,
           the promise and the light
           and the forgiveness?
Is there a life given also to me
        in the resurrection of Jesus Christ your Lord?

Is this your reason, in Jesus' words to you,
    "I have appeared to you for this purpose,
        to appoint you to serve and testify
           to the things in which you have seen me"?
Am I also to be such a witness?
    Would you have me show
        the power of personal experience?

Is there an excitement in the Christian life,
   such excitement that I would want everyone
      to know Christ's resurrection
      and what his resurrection
         has done for me?

You say he sent you
   "to open their eyes so that they may turn
      from darkness to light ...
      so that they may receive forgiveness of sins ...."
Paul, open your eyes and look at us!
Paul, I say it again, open your eyes and look at us!
   We're part of a twentieth century western
      civilization that has been losing its goals.
   We've moved so far from our roots in
      Christian faith and Christian morality,
         both personal and social,
         that some of our historians are calling this
            the post-Christian age.
   We don't need to look far
      for evidence of moral decay.
   But can we also see a light?
   Is there a light for us in your risen Christ?

You say that through Christ
   people may "receive forgiveness of sins ...."
Paul, you have the burden of those chains
   on your hands.
There are so many people in our century
   carrying heavier chains:
      chained to a load of guilt.
Can we believe the good news that you bear:
   that Christ breaks those chains,
      that he forgives,
         that he lifts the burden?
You say he offers
   "a place among those who are sanctified
      by faith in me."

We need a place.
    Everyone needs a place.
    Does your Lord offer us this place,
      a place in the family of God,
      a place in God's heart?

This is your experience, Paul.
    Is this what you want for us also:
      this hope you have found in Christ,
      this awareness of his love,
      this strength you have found in his strength,
        this glory in his resurrection?
    Do you want this same resurrection of Christ
      to give us power to live with renewed lives:
      lives of freedom and joy
      within our daily twentieth century pressures?
    Do you want us to feel
      that we are never alone again,
      for your risen Christ will be with us and in us?

Yes, Paul, you do not want us in prison as you are.
    Yet, jail or no jail,
      can we face anything and everything
        by the same power
          which raised Jesus from the dead?
    Will the same power which is at work in you
      be also at work in us?
Paul, do you want us to join you in praise,
    in hope,
      in thanksgiving to your risen Lord?

Why, Paul, why?
    Why would you have us be Christians?